"And they had then a notorious prisoner called Barabbas. So, when they had gathered, Pilate said to them, "Whom do you want me to release for you: Barabbas, or Jesus who is called Christ?" (Matthew 27:16-17 ESV)

# ATTICUS, 33 A.D.

## R.L. BARKER

Artwork by Elisha Schaff

# Table of Contents

| | |
|---|---|
| Saturday | V |
| Sunday | X |
| Monday | XVIII |
| Tuesday | XXXIV |
| Wednesday Morning | XLII |
| Wednesday Afternoon | LII |
| Thursday | LXIII |
| Friday | LXXVI |
| Friday Evening | CVII |
| Saturday | CXV |
| Sunday Morning | CXXI |
| Epilogue | CXXXII |

# PREFACE AND INTRODUCTION

*"I've always wondered about two particular men in the crucifixion story recorded in the New Testament Gospels – Barabbas who was released, and the unnamed Centurion who stood at the foot of the cross. What happened to them? Where did their story take them? From the research I've done, not much is known, so with the creative imagination given to me, I began to write.*

*I am not a historian by any means so I'm thankful for all the astute recorders who have already done the hard work to let me in on life in 33 A.D. Having been to Israel several times, I can only imagine it.*

*This is simply a story of what might have been, what could have been, and one day on the other side of this life, I will see how close I was to the truth of what actually took place."*

~ Rick Barker

# SATURDAY

The irons dug into his flesh, the blood dried and caked, but the wounds still painfully raw. He leaned his head back on the cold, wet rock behind him. That was it for his movement though. His legs were shackled numb, straight out in front of him, wrists in chains behind his back, and he was sitting awkwardly on the slimy rock floor, leaning sideways into the prison wall, which was hand-chiseled out of the side of Moriah.

He closed his eyes to the pain, both physically and mentally, and just breathed.

A stout leather-clad sentry stood at the cell door. He was Phoenician, barely understanding the language of Rome, but big enough that it did not matter much. He knew his job. He glanced at the prisoner and silently cursed this wretched place. A key in the main gate caught his attention and he straightened up, his hand on the hilt of his Roman *gladius* sword.

Light knocked back the darkness of the pit for a moment as the door swung open and two Legionnaires with blades drawn, marched a large brute of a man between them down the corridor to the cells. They shoved him forward despite his legs being bound by chain and his wrists tied with braided rope behind his back.

"Move pig!" one of the guards ordered the titan. He responded by spitting toward the soldier's feet.

That gesture was met with a flash of armor and a hard swing of the soldier's right arm, the hilt of his short sword hitting his target squarely above the left eye.

The blow broke the skin and caused the rugged rebel to reel backward a step, but only a step. He kept moving one foot in front of the other.

The Phoenician quickly unlocked the cell door in which the other prisoner stirred yet only enough to view the action with one eye open, the other shut. The door swung about, and Barabbas was thrown inside.

Atticus, the tall and lean armored soldier, a commander of 50, on the right of the prisoner, swiftly delivered a sharp blow with the flat of his blade on the back of his captive's head. It was a well-timed crack that sent the man stumbling forward into the rock wall before him, and with no way to stop his momentum, crashing headlong into the rock, breaking his nose and almost simultaneously sending him backwards to the stone floor.

Still bound with his hands behind his back, he was in too much pain and blurred shock to do anything but lay there as Atticus clasped an iron collar around his neck, effectively leashing him to an iron ring in the side wall.

"Just right for the dog you are," the other Roman said.

Both soldiers now moved with long-practiced ease, having locked down many Jews in this latest rebellion, then quickly took their leave, the Phoenician pulling the cell gate shut behind them, locking it with the loud clangor of metal on metal, and returning to his post, a small three-legged stool across the corridor.

Jonas turned with some difficulty to get a good look at Barabbas, the famed insurrectionist laying on the prison floor not three Roman paces away. The stench of blood and urine, feces, rats and rotting straw made him gag as he winced his way to a sitting position.

He had run with Barabbas before at Lachish and knew his reputation well, a reputation that was as accurate as it was ruthless and disturbing. He was not to be trifled with. The Romans were right to leash him. Even he would rather have the immense and carved rioter chained to the other side of the room with 15 feet between them than to risk the unpredictability of this bloodthirsty soul. Yes, he was a fellow Jew but he was also known to slay anyone who crossed his path regardless of ethnicity, though it was true that Jews fared better than most.

He adjusted his eyes to the light of the dawn now straining through the hole above them. Barabbas was out cold.

Jonas leaned back to the wall and sought sleep. It did not come.

His thoughts went to life outside the jail, knowing that it was his own foolish choices that led him to the spot he was now in. He recalled the last breath of freedom he had taken before the merchant started screaming at him, "THIEF! THIEF!"

Mayhem had broken out at that point and he ran for his life. He had been caught too many times by the Romans, beaten with rods, and even scourged with the short whip once – he did not want to go through that again.

It wasn't so much that he was a thief; that he knew well, but it was the fact he was such a bad thief who kept getting caught that bothered him most. Now he feared there may not be another chance given him.

# SUNDAY

Barabbas awoke madder than a cornered viper but could not do much about it except stand, crouch or take two steps to the right, two steps to the left, what with the metal leash around his neck. For now, the brawny insurrectionist just sat with his back against the wall, cursing Rome, the prison and anything else he could think of.

At 6'5" he was a head taller than most and rippling with muscle. He would always joke that he was of the tribe of Benjamin, a kickback to King Saul, the first King of Israel who was also a head taller than all – that is why he was so tall, he would say. Some believed him, most did not.

But he was a Benjamite, that he knew, born in Gibeah, the traditional territory of Benjamin and he took the words of his ancestor Jacob straight to heart – that Benjamin would be "a ravenous wolf; in the morning, he shall devour the prey, and at night he shall divide the spoil" (Genesis 49:27).

The tribe of Benjamin was notorious for its warlike nature and their fighting men had the reputation through the generations of being ruthless with a weapon, be it sword or sling, right handed or left. Barabbas fit the bill to perfection.

*Barabbas*, he thought. He cursed and mumbled, "Son of the Father... nothing like my father."

True, Barabbas or Bar- Abbas in the Aramaic tongue, literally meant Son of the Father but Barabbas was not at all like his father, a kindhearted man with a working farm north of Capernaum.

Barabbas quickly buried any thoughts of remorse for the pain he had caused his mother and father, and continued his cursing of the Romans whom he hated and blamed for all things. It is what he lived for, to kill Romans who were oppressing and occupying the land of his forefathers, the "Land of Promise."

He never saw himself as a Messiah figure but he did his best at trying to lead a true rebellion, a revolution of hatred against their despised conquerors. It was a revolution of hate, violence and rage and he was the natural leader.

His cellmate coughed and moved to a sitting position.

"Barabbas."
Jonas said his name again. "Barabbas"

Barabbas slow blinked a look toward Jonas.

"I was with you at Lachish... we took the Tenth Battalion... a mighty victory."

Barabbas looked at Jonas for a bit, studying him, then nodded once. Said nothing.

Jonas pressed further, "How did you... how did they get you?"

Barabbas, already tired of this conversation, said simply, "I was careless. Made too much noise at a tavern. Soldiers were marshalled."
Then recalling the scene with a slight smile, he added, "I think I stuck one though... doubt if he will live."

Jonas made every effort to get on Barabbas' good side - for too long as far as Barabbas was concerned - before deciding to lay low and mind his own.

Ω

Atticus moved quickly. On purpose. Being summoned by the Prefect was no light matter. It could only be bad news, perhaps an assignment to the far country of Gaul to put down a new rebellion, now that Rome had conquered the Celts, or to face more of the Parthian hordes in Armenia. Either way he would accept it, but not like it.

*Pontius Pilatus* was the fifth Prefect of the Roman province of Judea, serving as Governor under the Emperor Tiberius and for the most part, tired with his position. He would rather be in Rome. Though wearied with it all, he still garnered great respect from the Roman soldiers, mostly out of fear, because as a ruler he was known to be ruthless at times. And, he had also led his share of victories against their widespread enemies.

Atticus walked the corridors of the Prefect's 'palace', which was nothing more than an occupied Jewish estate, now filled with signs and emblems of the occupiers, the Roman Eagle, banners of the emperor and opulence everywhere. It was part of the Fortress of Antonia attached to the northwest wall of the Temple of the Jews.

He passed by two black-clad sentries of the Royal Guard as he rounded the last corner before the governor's residence. These were the personal protectors of Pilate and reserved elite for special duties.

Atticus punched his fist to his chest, the signal of allegiance to Rome, as he walked past them, receiving it back simply as a matter of duty and discipline.

He repeated the gesture as he entered the great hall and saw Pilatus look up at him from the maps.

The Prefect loved his maps, and studied them often throughout the day. He was Roman through and through and longed to return to the center of the then-known world. He dreamed of the Forum and the grand hippodromes, the gladiator competitions and ruthless politics of the Senate. He loved Rome. He stood up and immediately a servant moved toward him with a tray of food. He waved him off.

"Atticus Cornelius Julianus."

"Sir."

Pilate, as he was commonly known around Jerusalem, glided from behind the table of maps and miniature clay chariots, boats and men, and stepped toward a window overlooking the Court of the Temple. He wiped his hands on a towel the servant provided and then spoke. The servant moved to adjust the laurel but was again brushed aside.

"Atticus, your loyalty to the Emperor and to Rome travels well before you..."

Atticus did not respond – no response was needed - but waited for the assignment he was dreading. He enjoyed life as a soldier of Rome – as a commander of 50, he could do his duty, do as commanded and go home, a separate room at the barracks. The rabble rousers were generally put down rather easily; a few scuffles here and there - the food in Jerusalem never failed to satisfy, especially in the local markets, and other than the occasional run of a would-be Messiah, things were essentially calm.

"The winds of change are blowing, Atticus. We lost Marcus Didius in a tavern skirmish last night...was it last night? I do not recall…stabbed by a brute of a man, Barabbas." Atticus was aware of it, of course, having escorted the killer to the stocks the night before.

Still unsure of where his commander was heading, Atticus strained to anticipate what was next. He managed a nod but no words were leaving his lips yet.

The Prefect turned to face him.

"You will take his place Atticus. I am promoting you. You are now a Centurion of Rome, Commander of a hundred, in charge of the Third Cohort… Pleased? I am sure you are."

Atticus did not reveal the shock he felt inside; this was somewhat unusual, though not unheard of. Most Centurions were elected or appointed by the Senate but some were occasionally promoted from within the ranks for a variety of reasons besides their courage and loyalty – such as a fellow Legionnaire dying in the line of duty.

"Of course," said Atticus. "Pleased to serve Rome wherever I can, Prefect."

"Good." When there seemed nothing more to say, and an awkward silence lingered, Pilate said, "you may leave, Atticus. I will be seeing more of you I am sure. Report to the Third tonight and let your men know of the adjustment."

Atticus once more put his right fist to his heart, spun on his heels and exited.

He walked the long corridor toward the large double doors that opened to the portico and into the street.

He knew his pay would likely double and his living quarters would change. That he liked. He knew that Marcus' quarters were indeed splendid, overlooking the city and Temple.

The only downside, he thought, was that the Third Cohort, his new Command, governed over the ancient city itself, stationed all over Jerusalem, putting down rabble and rioters almost every day, especially on the Feast Days such as the upcoming Jewish Passover. You never know what to expect on Feast Days. An adventuresome life it was not, but it was not uninteresting either.

He made his way up the street to the general barracks, and to his room, thinking about this new challenge.

There were many parts of the military he disliked of course, but overall, he indeed was pleased and welcomed this new weight of responsibility.

He would tell his men of the change first thing in the morning.

# MONDAY

There was not much to do in this hell-hole but sit and think. And so, that is what he did.

Day 3 of serving his time moved along as slowly as Day 1 and 2, he thought. He looked at his shackles. At least the Phoenician had changed the position of the prisoners' hands from being cinched behind their backs to being somewhat useful in front again, though still in irons.

Everyone knew the slop they called food was not fit for a man, according to those who had to eat it. And, eat it he did, for Barabbas knew that if given the chance to escape, just one chance, he would need all his strength to do it.

Other than the welt above his eye, and a very sore nose, he was no worse for wear he thought, still strong, still able enough to crack a guard's head if need be. He looked at Jonas.

Poor man, Barabbas thought to himself. He squinted in the dark to see Jonas' form, to study it; "puny; could crush him with one hand."

"What is that you say?" Jonas asked, looking up from his bowl.

"Nothing," said Barabbas, "just thinking about… better days.

"Ah yes, well," Jonas held up his bowl of *prandium,* a meal-like goop consisting of a vegetable paste you might feed to a herd of pigs, "here is to better days. If we get out of here, there will be more of them… I am sure." He wanted to remain as positive as possible in any conversation with this oversized man.

Barabbas looked at him, leaned back against the wall and went again to thinking and dreaming of 'better days.'

He closed his eyes and he could see her, near the waters of the Galilee. It was her eyes that had grabbed his attention the first time he saw her. They were like two emeralds set in gold. She was serving drinks in a tavern at Magdala and her every move screamed for him to have her for his very own.

He was captivated by her walk, her glance, her smile. Though she wore a veil that night, he could tell she was smiling at him more than any others. That is what he believed. Her coal black hair cascaded over her shoulders reminding him of a flock of goats leaping down the slopes of Gilead, and framed her cheeks as if an artist had painted her portrait, just so.

He breathed deep, recalling her fragrance – what was it? Rose of Sharon? Frankincense? He let his mind drift to the first time they were together in Magdala; it felt like a lifetime ago but was so captivating that it made all the hatred of this day disappear, just thinking about it. He savored the memory. He knew if he got out of this fleapit, that he would go to her, to Magdala to the north, find her and maybe even marry her.

Magdala disappeared suddenly as he was jolted out of the Galilee by the heavy Phoenician, swinging open the cage again. Barabbas looked to see what now...

A third prisoner was being added to the mix as a single Roman guard, *pugio* dagger in hand, with the sharp point at the base of the man's neck, escorted him in. He was giving no trouble; he had been beaten badly and could barely walk, probably a broken knee cap by the look of it. The soldier simply pressed the dagger in close and nodded to a set of stocks in the middle of the floor.

The man got down with no little difficulty in front of the stocks and put his wrists into the bottom half of the contraption. The guard pulled him forward and flipped the top down on the man's forearms, painfully locking them down with a large pin bolt. Like his cell mates, he had been here before and knew the routine.

He was a thief, a murderer, one of the worst. Unclean through and through, rotten teeth and nasty disposition along with it. He was resigned right now to his fate as it would come. His knee shot pain up through his thigh right up into his face. He tried not to move.

"Execution for the lot of you," the Roman said, looking around the hovel and shaking his head in disgust. "Put you all out of your misery. That is what I recommend." Not that his recommendations would mean anything.
He turned and shoved aside the Phoenician with his elbow as he made his way out.

Jonas eyed the newcomer, did not recognize him but the light was still low and he thought maybe he knew him.
"You got a name?"

"Thief."

"No, that is my name," said Jonas, still doing his best at levity. His wrists still hurt. He winced. His legs were deadened with lack of circulation but he tried.

The man gave an effort at a laugh, more of a snort of an acknowledgement of some camaraderie, and then said, "Ethnan. That is my name."

"Welcome home, Ethnan," Jonas said. Ethnan grunted in response.

Barabbas did not want to enter this conversation at all. He closed his eyes again and tried to go back to

Magdala. But there was something happening outside the prison walls that he could not dismiss. A familiar commotion. The sound of riot. He knew it well. He led many, many encounters, always with an aim to take out at least one Roman, maybe two if he was lucky in a mob mentality. He generally succeeded. He was a master at stirring up a crowd and could ride the wave of increasing violence to the point of pulling a knife, sticking it in a Roman infantryman just under the armpit where the armored breastplate met back to front – in the exposed flesh. He would disappear into the swarming throng before the man would even meet the ground.

Indeed, a mob had gathered outside; he could hear it through the hole high above them in the man-made part of the wall. Two thirds of the wall were solid rock and a third was carved out and plastered.

This multitude had gathered on the Mount of Olives and had now worked its way down into the city. Another Messiah figure had risen, a man of Nazareth, Yeshua by name.

The streets were alive with shouts of his name and barking dogs; Barabbas could hear them clearly but still the sound was confusing to his ears. Nothing was being yelled out about Rome or Romans, nothing about mistreatment, not even the cruelty of oppression. All he could hear between blasts of the shofar, tandem hand-drums and loud tambourines was the repeated phrase, "Hoshiana" ~ Save! Save us!

Barabbas rolled his eyes and wanted to turn away from the clamor but could not escape it. "HOSHIANA! HOSHIANA!"

He knew the cry. It was Messianic. They were screaming about someone. Likely the Nazarene he had heard of, the miracle worker from Nazareth; he had not seen one himself, a miracle that is.

The miracle for him, he thought, would be the downfall of Rome, and a violent one at that. And to get out of this pit, he added in his own head as he looked around.

If this Nazarene would overthrow the oppressors, he would gladly be in there like a dirty sandal, fully throwing his weight behind his "kingship." But all he had heard about this man was a message of love – "now that would be a revolution," he grumbled out loud at the thought.

Outside the walls of prison, the triumphal shouts of the procession rose even louder as they passed by the holding cells on *Derech Hevron,* the road winding down from the top of the mountain, through the Kidron Valley and back up to the Zion Gate. The prison courtyard was also bordered by the street called Straight, named for its parallel path to the Cardo Maximus running north and south through the city.

Palm branches and cloaks were being thrown down in front of the would-be Savior, who was riding a young donkey, his men walking beside him, keeping the crowd back, taking it all in, and some leading the previously unridden animal. It was a jubilant celebration to say the least. However, Rome would not stand for it much longer if it grew any larger.

The Sanhedrin, those religious leaders of the Jews, the 71 as they were called, scattered throughout Israel, did not enter into all this victorious shouting, but they were there, and they were watching every move very carefully.

They were afraid of this man, Yeshua of Nazareth. He was different, always cornering them and besting them at their own game of cat and mouse questions. They feared for their position, prestige, and power over the people, even their influence with the Romans. This Nazarene would call them out in front of their people; it seemed to be a pastime of his, to bring reproach upon the title of Sadducee and Pharisee as often as he could. He would tell them their traditions were nullifying even the Word of G-d they proclaimed, that they were hypocrites like white-washed tombs, the blind leading the blind. These one-time heroes of the faith were slowly losing ground and were beginning to hate him for it.

At one point along the route, in a strange moment of near quiet as people simply breathed and walked along, one member of the council, Rueben ben Zereth, commanded the Teacher to "Silence your disciples. Rebuke them!"

The answer back was sharp as it was quick, "I tell you, if these were silent, the very rocks and stones would cry out," the Nazarene said.

Voices rose again in support of their new-found champion as the procession wound its way up through the city toward Jaffa.

The council continued to follow but at a distance and began to seriously plot the Nazarene's demise. Meanwhile, one of the Teacher's closest men lagged a little, stepping out of the shadows to engage them.

Ω

Atticus's warlike steed was a beautiful black stallion with an arrow of grey on its forehead, arrayed in Roman regalia, which commanded much attention as it high-stepped its way through the narrow streets of Jerusalem.

The sound of *Tonitrua's* hooves on the Jerusalem Stone simply added to its majesty. His trainer had named him Thunder for obvious reasons, thought Atticus as he surveyed the scene before him. The crowd was beginning to dissipate. The midday sun was too hot for them to continue their dance and he didn't blame them. He was seeking shade himself. The Jews fascinated him, worshipping one God alone when there were so many Roman gods to choose from.

There were gods of war, and agriculture, gods and goddesses of the stars, sky and water, gods of love and of planets – yet they choose to worship one God, whom they claim is the One and Only True God they called Yahweh, though they would not even let His name escape from their lips, they say, out of respect for The Name, and His Supremacy over all things.

Atticus watched as the revelry died down and people moved into the shade of the marketplace along the *Cardo Maximus*, the main street of the city always being worked on, lined with vendors from all nations. It was the hub of the people in his mind and always needed the strong presence of Rome.

And though they believe in this One True God as their Savior, they also keep holding to a promise that one day a Messianic leader will rise out of their ranks and win back their homeland, saving them even from Rome. Even here. He shook his head.

He dismounted Tonitrua and patted the massive equine's neck and cheek, gave him a rub on the forehead and walked toward a small shop, leading the big horse and looking for his favorite baked bread wrapped around roasted lamb with fresh dipping oil. The shop, no bigger than a small bedchamber, had many customers today, perhaps due to the celebration and festivity in the air, but as he approached, Aleixo whisked one of his teenage daughters into action to take care of his order first.

"Salutatio, my good sir," said Aleixo with a bow in his best attempt at Latin.

With a smile, Atticus responded with his best effort at Greek, "Kalo Apoyevma," a good day to you as well, my friend."

Aleixo, who had come to *Palestinia* from Cyprus seven years ago, served another customer while Atticus received his food from the youngest of the two daughters. He did not leave, however, for he had a purpose in lingering. Atticus had intentionally befriended the Greek, knowing that he was a valuable source of news and information in the city. He also found he genuinely liked the man, who felt like a fresh breeze blowing in over the Great Sea.

When many of the people had moved on, and business had slowed considerably, Atticus spoke again to Aleixo.

"Quite the parade we had today…"

"Yes," Aleixo said with new excitement in his voice. "It was for the Nazarene, Yeshua that is his name; he is quite amazing!"

"What do you mean, he is amazing? What is so amazing about him?"

Aleixo loved to wax eloquent and so he breathed deep and said, "He is a Rabbi of course. A Rabbi... yes, he teaches... but not like any other teacher. He speaks not like the scribes and not like the rulers of the law but with an authority that seems to... come from heaven itself!"

The barrel-chested Greek breathed deep again, clasped his hands together and said, "And, I was there Atticus – I was there, on a buying trip in Jericho, they have the best peppers I have seen in all of *Palestinia* in Jericho beautiful peppers of all colors – but I digress, yes, I was there minding my own business buying peppers when this Rabbi came through with his followers and a man born blind was healed right there in front me!"

"Healed? How do you mean?"

"Healed sir! He was blind, a beggar in fact, in ratted clothes, and then suddenly just like that he could see! Just like that! I was as close to him as I am to you now! The Teacher spoke over him, saying his faith had made him well, and immediately the man was healed!
"Did you see that he came by my shop today?" he added.

Atticus was intrigued by the healing. He had put down Messianic movements before. But he could not recall any such healing. "Did he say anything to you?"

"No, no…" He chortled. "But I was more than pleased that he looked my way. I felt the blessing of heaven just that alone."

"Hmm," said Atticus. A man who heals like this, and speaks with authority will need to be investigated further. A Jewish uprising on their Passover holiday would not sit well with *Pilatus*.

"Well, you have a good day Aleixo. I have much to attend to." He stepped back and swung Tonitrua's big head around, mounted him with some trouble, spinning round two times in the street before getting a hold. Once settled, he gave a nod of salute to Aleixo.

"Of course, of course," said Aleixo. "Any time I may be of service to you, my friend, just say the word." He bowed a big and graceful bow to Atticus.

Ω

Not far away, down through the *Cardo* and up a side street, Mariam of Magdala took time to rest. What a morning it had been! She gathered her thoughts under a small arch, a small pomegranate for her lunch. The Master was not far away, but busy with people bringing their children to him. He blessed them all.

She had a moment to herself. Not only had it been quite a morning, it had been quite a season, nearly four months of following him everywhere since her release from what she called her personal Hades. She closed her eyes and remembered what seemed so long ago, a life of men, grime, and slavery really, serving at the only Tavern of Magdala. A busy life indeed, a bad reputation, little to eat, little to celebrate.

Her body gave an involuntary shudder as she recalled the men, one after the other sometimes, that had their way with her, beatings from the Tavern keeper, the constant covering of her bruises, the drunkenness and the filth. Her life was more like a slave trap than anything; "whore" and "slave" were familiar names to her. She would not wish it on her worst enemy. But this was her life, the only life she knew.

Until he came along, and then everything changed. It was a day like any other when he came into Magdala on a preaching excursion from Capernaum. She heard him speaking in the square by the well, speaking new things to her ears about the Kingdom of God, lofty things too foreign for her. She left before he was done, and had gone into the market on an errand when she rounded a corner and ran nearly headlong into him and his entourage.

He said little but when his eyes met hers, they pierced her soul like nothing she had ever known before and she had known many men. Her longing for freedom from the many demons that held her captive was obvious and when the Teacher simply opened his arms, she did not hesitate. The embrace was not even long, but in it there came such a volcanic eruption of release of emotion – tears bursting from deep inside her, loud sobs, everything else disappearing from her senses – the crowd, the dust, the dirt, the grime, the market – all gone in the seconds of embrace and when she finally looked up at him, he was smiling a full, teethy, grin. She could not explain it, but her pain just seemed… gone. She followed him from that moment on.

Her days spent walking with the crowds, even in the heat of the afternoon were precious to her. Nothing could dampen her spirit. She could listen to him talk for hours and would go out of her way to bring him water or fetch something nourishing for him to eat. To somehow serve him, somehow bless him, was the least she could do. She felt strongly about that. History would call her a prostitute, a woman of "ill-repute," bad reputation. Truth be told, she was simply very broken and wracked by terrible abuse, both physically, emotionally and spiritually.

She opened her eyes and looked down at her dress, dirty yes, but not from men, not anymore; this was from the dust of the streets alone. She smiled. Her jewelry – what she had on her, she sold on Day 2 of her new-found freedom – and she realized had not even looked at an image of herself for the last three days! She gave a laugh at that. What a change this has been! She marveled at this man she now called Savior. Everything had changed. All because she had met him.

# TUESDAY

Barabbas was feeling stronger all the time. He felt he could almost break the chains that held his wrists and by leaning forward as much as he could strain, even the metal leash around his neck might pull away from the bolts in the rock-and-plaster wall behind him. He tested it again and again.

He could not stand the constant jabber of Ethnan and Jonas, who, over and over told stories of their personal conquests.

He learned Ethnan had a wife and family who lived in Tzzipori, Galilee's capital. The father of six little ones had ventured up to Jerusalem this week knowing that the Passover celebration would bring many opportunities for his 'trade'. He did not bargain, however, on being arrested when he tried his craft on a retiring and somewhat intoxicated Legionnaire. His own cockiness betrayed him, as the Legionnaire was not as drunk as he supposed. Before he had known it, Ethnan was laid out on a mosaic floor, waking up to a small band of soldiers surrounding him. His next stop was the prison he was now cursing.

"Curse this place and cursed be the sons of Remus… I hate the very smell of their breath…"

Jonas, yet unmarried but familiar with the ladies due to his quick wit and charm, was glad that he had no children in some distant region, waiting for him to bring home a Passover meal. His hometown of Hanikra was far to the north, on the coast of the Mediterranean where the white cliffs descend into the sea-washed *grottos*. So far from home, he thought. His mother and father were both still alive, his father a fisherman naturally, and his mother handcrafted and sold goods in the local markets. He had one brother, two sisters, the youngest still living at home. His brother had gone to Joppa to work in the boats, following in his father's footsteps and his other sister, Tabitha, had married and still lived in Hanikra.

He was grateful just to be alive, even if it was in this place, right now with this company. He was already thinking of what his next steps would be, where he would go once he got out. Joppa was the obvious choice, to see his brother Timaeus, and then maybe set sail to the west, to Greece, Spain, or to wherever the winds might take him.

He closed his eyes with a bit of a smile. Sleep came quickly for Jonas.

Ethnan cursed his captivity.

Barabbas stared into the darkness.

$$\Omega$$

It was nearly a full moon, a beautiful night as Atticus walked his new balcony overlooking the Jewish temple.

It had been a good day. He had dispersed the crowd of revelers, praising their new Messiah King, with relative ease. How nonsensical, he thought. There is no King but Caesar.

Following the crowd control exercise, which went extremely well due to the presence of Tonitrua, the stallion's mighty hooves stomping the stones, and head bouncing up and down ready to engage in battle. Tonitrua had saved Atticus much work.

The afternoon had gone quickly as he oversaw his move into the new quarters, already furnished with some of the best décor of Rome thanks to Didius having lived there for more than a year. The residence boasted a great room with a magnificent sleeping chamber off to one side, a servant's room on the other, a preparation place for food and drink, and to Atticus' shock and delight, indoor plumbing and a personal bath area! He smiled at the thought of not needing to use the public toilets anymore for he feared what might crawl out of those wretched sewers! Private latrines were becoming more and more common all the time, even in the older parts of the city. His was not dependent on the public sewer, though, which was the way he liked it... because of his suspicion of sewer... things. There were things of the unknown that he feared, since childhood, things that no one knew about.

A personal latrine was new to him and he began to think about how it works, where the waste and water goes. He also did not like the public bath houses, even though they were a customary place of business, because he felt the heat and steam was a perfect breeding ground for parasites, lice and worms. He avoided the ritual cleansings as much as possible as long as he could also avoid the offense of simply not being there.

But looking around, his favorite part of his new dwelling was his terrace overlooking the city. He enjoyed it in the early morning before the city awoke, and he enjoyed it at night when a sense of peace veiled what lay beneath.

He took in the sights this night, torches lit on the Temple walls, the flicker of candlelight in the homes in the valley, and up the Mount of Olives, the moon amid misty clouds. He stared at the Jewish Temple for a few moments.

What a magnificent structure, he thought, admiring the architecture and the sheer enormity of it. The arches and pillars of the portico were of incredible craftsmanship. If nothing else, he thought, Herod the Great lived up to his name in building. He wondered if Solomon's Temple had truly been more stunning.

He pondered what Aleixo has told him about this new upstart leader of the Jews. Was he any different than all the rest? Could there be something to all this talk? What was wrong with the Roman gods? The Greeks had many too; what was wrong with them? His thoughts swirled. While he prayed to his personal god, Mars, god of war, spring and justice, patron of the Roman Legions and divine father of Romulus and Remus, he realized he had not had many answers to his prayers over the years. But then again, look at his surroundings! He did have what seemed to be some favor, which he supposed to be of Mars… or Venus, the mistress of Mars whom he called upon on occasion.

He shook his head as if pulling out of a spider web of thoughts, lifted his goblet of fine wine from the mountains surrounding Jerusalem, and toasted Mars in the sky before he drained it for the second time that evening.

He placed the goblet on the balcony ledge, savoring the last drop, and walked away, aiming for his chambers. Dawn comes early, he thought, lots to do. He wondered about seizing one of the scribes or rulers of the law in the morning and asking him more pointed questions about this so-called Messiah. Yes, that is what he would do.

Having dropped his light armor onto the floor and now just in his white tunic, he lay still on his bed, thinking and listening to the night sounds. The wine began to take deeper effect and he started to drift.

Suddenly, he was aware of someone else in the room; he bolted upright and grabbed his *pugio,* a leaf-shaped short blade from the table near the bed.

The man at the foot of his bed was large. Atticus could not see his hooded face. He rose from the bed, dagger in hand.

"Who are you? How did you get in here? In the name of the gods of Rome, answer me!"

The man did not answer but held out a scroll. Atticus felt uneasy but not in danger and he stared at the man. He found himself slowly reaching for the scroll being held out to him. It was almost as if he was compelled to take it, compelled to look at it. In fact, he could not resist.

As he reached for it, he saw written in Hebrew the letters זכריה and he realized he had no idea what it meant. He looked at the man, whose clothes began to shine. And as he looked at him, the letters, which formed a single word, rushed at him from the scroll like a charging lion might, growing larger as it drew closer to his face.

He awoke with a start and found himself on the marble floor of his chamber.

"A dream!" He cursed, catching his senses. He breathed deeply and felt the wine again as the room started to tip up and to the left. "Ahh, yes," he said, "good wine."

He climbed back onto his bed and tucked his face into the pillows with a groan. He thought for a moment about the man with no face and shiny clothes, touched the hilt of his *pugio* dagger, assured that it was indeed still at his side in its sheath where it should be, glanced once to the foot of his bed, and drifted off to sleep.

# WEDNESDAY MORNING

J onas had new hope.

He remembered something this morning that stirred a new sense of optimism and courage at the possibility of getting out of this rat-infested pigsty.

Passover. There was a tradition at Passover that sometimes a prisoner would be released if the Governor was in a good mood. He felt maybe, just maybe, since his behaviour had been cooperative enough with the Romans that he stood a good chance of being set free as a gesture of good will from the Roman Procurator to the Jewish people at their biggest feast of the year.

He would not say anything to Barabbas or Ethnan about this; he did not want to alert them to the possibility and they be freed in his stead, but he would remain hopeful over the next two days and do his best to make a good impression - even on the Phoenician when he served the once-a-day meal.

Meanwhile, Barabbas had been working the ring bolts to the point that one good wrench of his full weight against the plastered wall behind him would turn his leash into a deadly weapon, still a ring around his neck but a chain with a hefty slab of iron on the other end of it that he could swing into the jaw of an unsuspecting enemy. He began to make plans.

Once he took out the Phoenician with his slab-and-chain, he would simply use the jailer's keys to unlock the outer door, use the guard's own *spatha*, a triangular-bladed short sword, to dispose of any other sentries he would be privileged to surprise in the corridor. He smiled at the thought of it all coming together.

Timing would be crucial as to not attract more attention than necessary. Timing. Yes, he would wait until tomorrow evening, the night before the Passover Shabbat when the city started to quiet; the Romans would be even more lazy than usual, he thought, and unsuspecting that anyone would ever even try to breach this pit. At evening tomorrow, yes, when sup was served, he would do it. And he knew his plan would work. Nothing could stop it. Should he let them in on it?

He looked over at Ethnan and Jonas. A pathetic pair, he thought. Though Ethnan might be a reasonably good ally in a scrap with some Roman guards, these two prison pals would probably be more of a liability to him than help. He decided to keep his plans to himself and just worry about breaking free of the wall first, and then taking out the Phoenician at "dinner time" tomorrow night.

Having been taken out of the stocks the day before and linked into a leash very much like Barabbas,

Ethnan now used his left foot in a mad attempt to crush a nearby rat but he let out a scream of pain as his right knee erupted once again. He fell against the wall in agony and watched the rat scuttle past him and out the cell door.

"Pathetic," said Barabbas.

Ω

Atticus rose early and went immediately to the stables to greet Tonitrua. This would be his new routine as a Centurion; he never had a horse to think about before and now he wanted to develop a good relationship of trust knowing that when it came to charging a horse through angry crowds, anything could happen; anything could spook it. And, since he was not the best of riders, he wanted Tonitrua, as well-trained as even the mount of Caesar, to know and trust him very well. As a commander of 50, he had a horse allotted to him, but he never rode.

The stables were nothing more than a converted bathhouse – it is hard to keep a horse in the city, let alone a dozen, which is what the Third Cohort had here. The commanders of 50 and of 25 each had their own if they chose, and then there were the younger horses being trained. Atticus walked into the stall row whistling, which brought some of the horses to their gates snorting and stomping. Tonitrua was in the second to last stall and was up at once, flipping its ears, snorting and stomping like the rest of them –not so much with excitement at seeing its new owner but more to do with the onslaught of the flies.

Atticus drew close to the gate, which came up to his chest and rubbed Tonitrua on the grey patch of its forehead. He dug into his satchel and brought out a small ripe apple he had plucked on the way to the stables, holding it out for Tonitrua to devour, its head bobbing in what seemed like extreme gladness.

Atticus stayed with Tonitrua for a short time before heading down the steep side street leading all the way from the Jaffa Gate down to the Gate called Beautiful, near the Temple.

He stopped off at a morning shop for cut wine – wine diluted with water and honey -- and spoke with a half-dozen of his men about security plans for the Passover. Everything needed to be tightened up when the city swelled with devoted Jews from all over *Palestinia,* not to mention those coming from other countries as far away as Syria and Egypt. The city was already beginning to feel the strain of extra bodies, with inns and eating establishments bursting at their seams with combustion.

Even his walk this morning felt more pressed than usual, thought Atticus, having to bump and push his way through many outsiders carrying satchels, leading small caravans of kids and animals, presumably for sacrifice, he guessed. Not the kids of course, but the animals.

He did not like it. He did not like it as a foot soldier, nor as a commander of 50, and now as a commander with the charge of the whole inner city, he was more than just a little aware of the tension he felt inside himself, let alone all around him. One could almost cut it with a knife.

He picked up two more of his men and bade them to follow as he made his way down to Bethesda by the sheep gate. The rulers of the law often gathered there and he wanted to talk with one or possibly two of them to find out more about the Hebraic beliefs in a Messiah.

The Temple loomed ahead and he could make out something, trouble brewing perhaps. A crowd was gathering.

"Look lively, men," he said to the two, and they all quick-paced it together, hands on hilts, ready to draw swords if necessary.

Mariam was pressing in closer as the Teacher was looking directly at the chief priests and scribes while telling a parabolic story about some men of a vineyard who murdered the son of the owner. He was asking them a question but did not expect an answer: "What then is this that is written: 'the stone that the builders rejected has become the cornerstone?'

"Everyone who falls on that stone will be broken to pieces and when it falls on anyone, it will crush him."

The teeth-grinding scribes did not even attempt an answer but Mariam could see they were consorting with the chief priests about how best to lay hands on the – she heard the words "troublemaker" and "blasphemy" because they perceived he was pitting his parables purposefully against them. *They fear the people*, thought Mariam, *and so they should.*

Yeshua was indeed rising in popularity, especially after the big entry into the city. They would watch him and even send in spies, who, pretending to be sincere, would try to catch him in saying or doing something against the Law of Moses so they could deliver him up to the authority and jurisdiction of the Governor to have him put away.

Atticus and now four Legionnaires, two of which had pushed through to the front of the crowd with their shields leading the way, were part of the listening audience. For the first time, Atticus saw the man they were calling Teacher, Messiah, or Master. He looked him up and down. Studied him. He had no weapon in his tunic that he could see, unless it was well hidden, and not a trace of anger did he wear on his face; Atticus had seen a million angry men and knew instantly that this was not a man of violence. He was well aware though, that the mob on the other hand could turn on a coin so he was still very cautious and very alert. He tilted his head to squint against the morning sun to look more closely at this Yeshua, who he felt looked almost preoccupied with a child wanting a hug. He looked again to the priests and their tag-along scribes. One of the scribes lifted his voice to address the Preacher.

"Teacher, we know that you speak and teach rightly, and show no partiality among the people, but truly teach the way of G-d…"

Atticus sneered, recognizing the tongue of a lying man, religious or not. There was no way they believed this man was teaching the way of God, even if he was.

"Is it lawful for us to give tribute to Caesar, or not?" the scribe put it to Yeshua and awaited his response.

*Crafty*, thought Atticus. *This should be interesting. If he answers no, then Rome would be obligated to deal with him; if he answers yes, then he could lose favor with the people who are bitter against their oppressors.*

"Show me a denarius," the Preacher called out, and people began looking for a coin. It was Atticus himself, now fully engaged in this contest, who tossed one high into the air toward Yeshua, who snatched it out of the air.

"Whose likeness and inscription does it bear?" He showed it. "Whose image is on the coin?" he asked of the scribe, whose answer was a quick, "Caesar's."

He said to them, "then render to Caesar what is Caesar's and to G-d what is G-d's."

Even the scribes seemed impressed with this answer, which shut them up for the moment and they went back to their collusion. Atticus was impressed as well.

A man standing beside Atticus said to another, "…and if it is G-d's image upon us, then what is it that we should render to G-d… but ourselves!"

The Roman looked down at the speaker, who was smiling as if fairly caught up with his own wisdom. Atticus slow-blinked his way back to the Teacher. But he was gone. He had already moved off the steps he was sitting on and was now heading out toward the marketplace.

Atticus overheard him tell his followers, "beware of the scribes, who like to walk around in long robes, and love greetings in the marketplaces and the best seats in the synagogues and the places of honor at the feasts, who devour widows' houses and for a pretense make long prayers. Theirs will be the greater condemnation."

L

Aleixo was right, he thought. He does speak with an authority unlike what he has heard from any teller of tales or teachers before. He took note that this is a man worth monitoring very carefully, and that his enemies will not suffer him long.

He motioned to his men. "Follow him today. See if he is a disturber of Jerusalem or if he is harmless. If he speaks against Rome, we will take him in for questioning at the least, perhaps dissuade him, or evict him from the city if need be."

They snapped their right fist to their chests on cue as one and followed the trailing crowd. Atticus turned to the scribes.

"You there." He pointed one out, all of them looking shocked as if perhaps they unknowingly did something wrong. "You. Come to me."

The Pharisee, seemingly a few years above the rest as far as Atticus could perceive, stood up from his perch, and looked at the others. They shrugged and nodded their approval and some motioned with their eyes to cooperate with the Roman. He stepped over to Atticus.

"Walk with me."

# WEDNESDAY AFTERNOON

LII

"**Y**our name?"

Nicodemus was unsure whether to answer him fully but remembered the glance of his brothers to obey the Centurion. So, he told him his name and a little bit more.

Atticus began his questioning of the ruler, a member of the Sanhedrin, schooled in the law and the prophets of the Hebrews, a rabbi in his own right, a teacher of the Jewish people.

He questioned him about the Messiah, first from the scribal point of view, and of the Pharisees and then his own personal standpoint, specifically what he felt about this upstart, Yeshua of the Galilee.

They walked and stopped, and walked some more, spent a good two hours together.

"We have awaited the *Mashiach*, the Messiah or Anointed One, whom the Greeks call the Christ, for thousands of years," Nicodemus told him. "The books of history, the prophets - the Torah - all foretell of his coming."

He told Atticus of the prophecies of *Ysha'yah* (Isaiah) son of Amoz, of how the prophets *Mikah* told of his coming, the Psalms, the books of history detailing he would be a descendant of David, the second King of Israel, yet the Son of G-d, the Ancient of Days, even to the place of his birth in the tiny village of Bethlehem yet also to be known as a Nazarene coming out of *Netzer*, the branch of the stump of Jesse.

"So, what about you? Do you believe all these prophecies?" asked Atticus.

"Of course," Nicodemus replied. "There is no question of my faith in the Torah as G-d's truth.

"And what about this Yeshua – does he fit into these prophecies?"

"That is another question…" Nicodemus stroked his long beard. "We are still not sure. Some of the scribes, a few Pharisees and even some of the Sadducees are beginning to say, 'yes' he is the One, but for me that is almost too remarkable to be true, that G-d would visit us here in our day and in our time. Most of us are still trying to understand."

Then he paused and said, "And, some want him gone."

"Gone?" Atticus stopped walking and demanded, "What is your meaning?"

Nicodemus thought perhaps he had gone too far but knew now he had to give an answer of some kind. "There is talk of his demise. One of his disciples has already met with some of our leaders and may be open to, shall we say, a turning of the tide. He is soft and wants his Master to do something extraordinary, to stand up and face Rome and bring his kingdom into existence. It would not take but a handful of silver to persuade him... to be the trip-wire of... an occurrence, let us say."

Atticus understood, and started walking again. He queried further, "You speak in riddles. Who can stand up to the might of the Roman empire?"
No one spoke for twenty paces. Then knowing that he had already alluded to this, Atticus asked again, "What about you? Do you believe in this Yeshua as Messiah?"

Nicodemus swallowed. Atticus noticed. Nicodemus picked up the pace a bit. Atticus matched him. Crowds were still pouring into the city, even as the sun began to drop in the late afternoon sky.

"Almost."

"Almost?" said Atticus.

"I talked with this prophet, some call him a prophet, a year ago... today, yes a year ago today! And I was taken like the rest with his ability to heal the lame, to make blind men see..."

"I have heard of this healing power, some magic perhaps?" Atticus said.

"No, no, it is of G-d I believe, but how he does it I do not know. I saw him heal a leper once making a man's face go from large leprous wounds to being soft as a babe's – in an instant. It was a miracle from heaven, no question.

"And, he speaks with wisdom, as you saw back there. Still…" Nicodemus stroked his beard again and hesitated.

"What?" Atticus was more and more intrigued all the time.

"Still, I cannot give myself to surrender fully to his way of thinking. Now, no one can do the things he does, without G-d being with him, but he spoke to me that night about being born anew and I could not follow him then, and I still do not understand now. He said unless a man is born twice he cannot even see the Kingdom of G-d – cannot even see it?! I asked him then, 'how is it that we go back into our mother's womb? And, he told me unless one is born of water and the Spirit, he cannot enter the Kingdom of G-d – now I cannot enter? How can these things be?!" Nicodemus was raising his voice.

Atticus just looked at him intently but said nothing. Nicodemus sighed, "he has spoken many other things, some very difficult to understand. He also wondered at me being a teacher of Israel if I do not understand these things. So, in answer to your question, my mind is not made up. I will continue to discern and trust G-d to tell me what I need to know."

They were at the crossroads of Straight and the Street of Chain, more of a cutaway alley than a Roman street, and Nicodemus indicated he needed to part. Atticus sincerely thanked the man for taking as much time to speak with him as he did and bade him a good evening, "Erev Tov," he said.

"Shalom," replied Nicodemus, bowing slightly and then hurrying off as the evening faded into the sunset behind the Jerusalem hills.

As Atticus turned to head to his own quarters, he suddenly remembered his "encounter" the night before at the foot of his bed. Ahh, he realized he could have asked Nicodemus about the Hebrew word that "attacked him" in his dream. He looked back to see if he could see him but there was no trace of him in the multitude of people. Nicodemus was long gone.

Ω

Mariam let loose the water jar into the well, listening for the familiar sound of it hitting the water; she let it sink deeply and then drew it back to the top. She was worried. The conversations and challenges of the day seem to have intensified even more since the last Shabbat. The celebration of the Master's entrance into Jerusalem seemed so distant now, and he talked of death, and suffering, and rising again.

She had seen the plots of men before and she felt something was stirring.

"Do you need a hand, dear lady?" the gravelly voice interrupted her train of thought.

"Oh... no thank you," she said, turning to see who it was offering assistance. Judas, one of the Lord's closest followers. He was of the north country and rumored to have been part of the *Sicarii*, a cadre of rebels intent on taking down Rome. Judas had been with the Teacher from the beginning, almost three full years of ministry.

He touched her arm and she pulled back and lifted the water jar up over the ledge. She did not trust him. She could not pin the reason; it was just a feeling.

"Laila Tov... how are you, this fine evening?" he said with a show of his pearly white teeth.

She breathed deep in obvious frustration and said she was well. She was about to leave when he asked her a pointed question.

"When do you think Yeshua will make his move?"

"I am sorry, I do not understand," she said.

"I am just wondering when he will do it, you know, set up his kingdom. He seems to be waiting for something, a very patient man he is," Judas said, looking off into the moonlit night as if trying to pull his next thoughts from the stars. "I think it should be soon though. Things seem right... he has the favor of the people. Rome is agitated but their eyes are elsewhere in faraway battles. It just seems... right."

"You should simply ask him," said Mariam, who then used the following moment to escape. "He has asked for a drink. I need to go to take this to him. Laila Tov."

"Yes," Judas said. "Laila Tov."

Ω

The Phoenician stirred a pot of weak stew over an open fire, tasting it with a satisfied nod of his head. If it was good enough for him, he thought, it was good enough for them.

He poured the slop into three bowls and served up dinner to his captive scum. He hated this "job" but then again it was all he had. In some ways, they were all he had.

Jonas surprisingly thanked him, still trying to stay on his good side, aiming for that Passover lottery possibility. He had whispered his idea to the Phoenician yesterday and thought maybe there was hope he was getting through. As far as the

Phoenician knew, Jonas was talking about his fine cooking.

Ω

Atticus moved quickly through the labyrinth of alleys as street torches were being lit. He hurried to make it to Aleixo's eatery before he shut it down for the night.

As he worked his way through the congested streets and tucked into various shortcuts, a scuffle broke out in front of him, spilling over from an argument inside a public house.

One man was spitting curses at two others. "Fool," thought Atticus as he drew near. Suddenly one member of the duo charged the fool and two danced in a pressure on pressure embrace, and then the other entered the fray and rained down blows upon the fool's head and neck.

With surprising wisdom, the fool brought his knee up into the groin of his first attacker, which sent him blenching to the ground and his partner had some second thoughts about continuing the brawl.

Atticus yelled, "take it off the streets! Away with you or you will end up in my care!" He pushed between them continuing to move along his pathway up a short, steep incline. Just around the corner was Aleixo's.

The fool had fallen to the street at the strength of Atticus' forearm push and the other just startled, quickly pulled at his friend's tunic and the two scrambled back into the Roadhouse, out of the way.

Atticus rounded the corner and saw Aleixo's daughter working at the shutters.

"Good evening," he said, "Is your father nearby?"

"He is," the young gal replied. "I will get him for you."

His dream the night before seemed to be pursuing Atticus now, the thought of the Hebrew letters racing toward his face kept coming back at him. He had written them down after his talk with Nicodemus and wanted now to show Aleixo, who appeared in the doorway with a hearty good greeting.

"Aleixo, I want to know if you can help me out with a puzzle," Atticus said, pulling the piece of parchment from his satchel.

Aleixo, always up for a game, studied the handwritten script זכריה and said, "it is Hebrew."

"This I know," said Atticus with a little impatience. "I am just not sure what it says. I think it is a name," Atticus tilted his head and stooped a bit to hear Aleixo better in the din of the passersby.

"Yes, indeed it is a name but it is also a prophet, and it is also a scroll... it is Zechariah. What does it mean, Atticus?"

"Well I do not know if it means anything at all. Just a name perhaps. Merits be to you once again, my friend."

Aleixo then offered Atticus a cup of cut wine, but Atticus thought the better of it, bid him a good night and carried on up the street toward his quarters.

In an olive grove not far away, a man walked and quietly prayed alone on a terraced hill. In silence and solitude, he found strength. Drained from the day's wrestling match with leaders of the law, of decisions made, and people pressing in on him for more, from dangers of ambush attempts by the spies of the Pharisees, and simply the weight of desperate souls, he sought and found rest. He sought and found peace. He sought and found communion with the Hebrew G-d, Yahweh, the One he called Father.

# THURSDAY

A rooster resounded its raucous morning wake-up call somewhere in the recesses of Atticus' mind, and distant though it was, it did begin to pull him out of his state of death called sleep into waking life once again.

He arose cursing the cock that crowed and broke fast with a traditional daybreak meal called *ientaculum*, a flat round loaf made of emmer grain, eggs, cheese, honey, fruit, olives, and cut wine. All this was prepared daily by a servant who would rise even earlier to get to one of some 33 bakeries in the city before laying out the dish for the morning. Atticus was not faithful to the meal, however, especially on a day like today when he already felt he was behind, having slept too long, and with much to do.

He pulled his mail shirt on and then a light armor breastplate this morning, sheathed his gladius on his right side near the short blade, strapped high leather boots that came up to just below the knee, and went out to the overlook terrace, breathing in deeply the crisp morning air.

A small flock of turtle doves fluttered up from the flat-roof house below him on his right and the streets were already awakening with sounds of merchants opening shutters and yelling across the street to one another, dogs barking, even some morning prayers being lifted. A mule let off a wild bray in the distance. The cock crowed again. Atticus took a sip again from his morning's fuel, thanked the gods and turned to face his day.

He moved with an objective through the streets to the barracks of the Third Cohort. Today, tomorrow and the next day would be exceedingly busy. When he arrived at the barracks he marshalled his VI to the morning symposium where he gave clear orders for the coming days. Passover was upon them whether they liked it or not; streets were full. There would be festivities, and out of those festivities, there would be drunkenness, and therefore, fights, and other petty crime.

"You and your men will be up for the task by my Mars or I will have you put in the stocks first, followed by your lazy men! Clear?"

They hit their chests in unison. "Sir!"

The four leaders of 25 were given quadrants of the old city to oversee, while the two 50s commanders were posted on the northern and southernmost gates, Damascus to the north near the Rock, and the Zion Gate on the southern slope overlooking the Hinnom Valley. Atticus would convene at midday with the two commanders of 50 at the Temple Mount for further orders. Each gave their salute to Caesar before departing on their way.

It was a short walk to the stables where Atticus received Tonitrua, having been already washed, fed, prepped and tacked for the day by the stable master's crew.

Tonitrua was more than ready to run, and it did not take long to cross the Kidron and ascend the Mount of Olives toward the house of the only Rabbi he knew in the city personally – Nicodemus.

Nicodemus was fit for his age. At 62 years, he had seen his share of hard days, but all the walking throughout Israel over his years and in the last decade on Jerusalem's hilly roads, kept him agile and swift.

He was not expecting a Roman Centurion to knock at his door so early in the day. He had just finished his morning Shema and was sitting down to a piece of flatbread and olive oil when the 'thump, thump' of the 'hand of Rome' hammering at the door, broke the silence.

Nicodemus first looked out a small look-see cut into the mortar and seeing the sun reflect off Tonitrua's bronze-plated breastplate, he knew who was about to grace his morning.

With a quick maneuver of the bolt, and a pull of the door, Nicodemus welcomed Atticus into his home, offering him a piece of his flatbread. He was curious as to how Atticus knew to find his place of lodging, what with the tendency of rabbis to move around, often staying at different schools of the Torah throughout the city. Atticus quickly brought that curiosity to an end with a simple "Rome" as he removed his crimson-plumed helmet and tucked it under his arm. He passed on the flatbread. Nicodemus moved on to other things.

"What brings you to my little abode?" he asked.

"This," spoke Atticus and pulling the note from a pouch in his belt, he showed Nicodemus the Hebrew word he now knew was Zechariah.

"Are you looking for a man or a scroll?" Nicodemus prodded as he poured water from a flask into two cups. He dropped a piece of citrus into each.

"You tell me," said Atticus taking the cup, and then proceeded to give as much detail as he could from his dream encounter of two nights ago. He told him of the man at the foot of the bed - he could not recall his face - of the scroll he held out, and "so yes, maybe a scroll, that just occurs to me now," and how the man's clothes began to shine when the Hebrew word rushed toward his face and awakened him with a start.

He wondered why he was being so overly open with his dreams to this man he barely knew, but he was after all a priest of some kind and maybe he knew something that would be valuable in his investigation of this Messiah man. He caught himself recalling Yeshua silencing the leaders with just a question.

Nicodemus sipped his water and savored it for a moment before getting up from his chair in the little kitchen area and disappearing into another room.

Atticus took the moment to look around at his surroundings for the first time, which were humble to say the least. Small food preparation area, several baskets hung from the wall, apparently one or two rooms were adjacent to this sitting place. Nicodemus returned.

In his right hand were several scrolls, in his left just one. He put the many down on the table between them, and then took the one, untied it and unfurled it with careful meticulousness.

"This," he said, "is the scroll of Zechariah, the one in your dream. I copied this myself years ago while at Herod's summer palace in the south, except it was winter."

Atticus got up from his chair and joined Nicodemus at the hip, scrutinising the text. It meant nothing to him; he could not read Hebrew.

"What is it saying?" Atticus asked him.

Taking an ivory Torah *Yad*, a traditional Jewish pointer, which literally means 'hand' and even had a carved finger at the tip of it, he began to trace along the words, reading aloud from right to left the portion he had randomly rolled it out to.

*"Rejoice greatly, O daughter of Zion! Shout aloud, O daughter of Jerusalem! Behold, your king is coming to you; righteous and having salvation is he, humble and mounted on a donkey, on a colt, the foal of a donkey."*

Both gave a small gasp of realization as they heard the phrase spoken aloud in the quietness of the morning air between them. Yeshua had ridden into the city on a colt.

Ω

"Then Judas Iscariot, who was one of the twelve, went to the chief priests in order to betray him to them. And when they heard it, they were glad and promised to give him money. And he sought an opportunity to betray him."

(The Gospel of Mark 14:10-11 ESV)

Ethnan felt his escape plan was working perfectly and the time had come to implement it fully. Escape had always been on his mind, unbeknownst to his fellow inmates.

His knee, though still painful, was usable and he found that if he pressed in as close to the wall as possible behind the cell door itself, he would have about five feet of chain link, with which he could choke the life from the Phoenician and make good a run to freedom. He had not spoken of this to Barabbas nor Jonas because he felt they might talk him out of it, or turn him in – and neither would suit him.

It was nearing the time of the evening sop and he could hear the Phoenician at the fire. It would not be long.

Barabbas, meanwhile, had his own plot racing through his mind and it would also go down at meal time.

Ethnan could hear the portly guard ambling toward the cell. He pressed himself in tight to the wall, readying himself by pulling up as much length of chain as he could muster. Barabbas was not paying attention to him, otherwise he may have done something to avert what took place next, having in mind his own plan of action also about to be taken.

The door opened and Ethnan sprang into combat, albeit too soon. There was no way he could have even touched the Phoenician, who, though somewhat obese, could still move quickly if need be, which he did.

He threw the bowls directly at the would-be assassin, who screamed like a tiny girl as the burning lumps of whatever it was stuck on to his arms, chest and face. Then the guard deftly grabbed his cat-o'-nine-tails whip from its home in his belt and gave a rapid swash of the leather across Ethnan's face. Ethnan reeled back in pain as the bits of bone and rock, sewn into the leather cords, ripped a piece of flesh from his cheek.

The Phoenician yelled obscenities in his native language, which no one could understand, and gave another lash of his scourge for good measure as Ethnan cowered in the corner against the back wall. Tucking the weapon back in his belt, the foreigner yelled something at Jonas and Barabbas, who were standing stunned, and closed the door behind him, bolting it loudly as he went.

Jonas looked at the empty bowls on the floor amidst the rotting straw. There would be no food tonight, at least not for them. The rats will be happy, he thought to himself.

Barabbas could not believe what just happened. He stood at his chain, silent for the moment, straining against the wall. He then let out a yell that would send a pack of jackals scattering.

"IDIOT!" His own plan thwarted for now, he would have to wait until the morning.

Ω

Atticus had dispatched the *speira*, a small band of soldiers as ordered by Pilate, just when it was nearing the second watch of the night; he limited the number to 12, as it was simply to quell any potential rioting that might occur with the arrest that was to be made tonight by the high priest's guards.

The Legionnaires did not often partner with the officers of the temple of course, but it was not unheard of either, especially if it was to put down a suspected revolution. It was a fragile arrangement at best and tenuous always. But apparently, according to the High Priest Caiaphas and his ring of leaders, a revolution was indeed at hand and needed to be quelled once and for all, or Rome would be under siege before they knew it. The Messianic promises of this Nazarene carpenter, the power of the people acclaiming him, the signs and wonders that had the city astir, all pointed to the necessity of making an arrest as soon as possible, considering too, the Passover celebration upon them.

Pilate had given the priests the small speira earlier in the night and Atticus now stood on his balcony looking toward the Mount of Olives in the light of a strikingly full moon. It was reported that this was where the Preacher would be with his men, the

Garden called Gethsemane. Trouble was brewing. He could feel it. Blood may be spilled tonight, he thought. He leaned on one elbow, resting his chin in hand and listened intently for any sound of violence.

Torches lit up the Garden as the speira, a group of officers of the Temple, several of the priests, and their personal servants snaked their way into the darkness of the grove led by the man called Iscariot, one of the closest followers of the Nazarene. The sign which marked his Master would be a kiss of betrayal by this man, Judas.

There was a minor scuffle when many of the group of believers scattered and one man, the big fishermen, struck out with a short fishermen's blade and took the ear from the head of Malchus, the servant of the high priest. It was said later, that the blow was misdirected, as the fisherman had wanted to do more than just wound the man. But the Galilean leader commanded Shimon, as he was called, to put away his sword, picked up the ear of Malchus from the brush below him and placed it back on the side of his head, as if something like that happened every day. From that moment in the Garden that night, it was stunned silence as the Preacher held out his wrists to be bound and was led out of the grove toward the house of Annas, the son-in-law of the High Priest Caiaphas. It was well after midnight when this happened. Atticus had fallen asleep and slumbered the entire time the drama unfolded.

Once bound, the Temple Officers and even the soldiers got in on roughhousing their captive, throwing random blows to his face, kidney and torso area. The rest of his followers fled into the night after Malchus, who was still holding his hand to his head in sheer shock, had been healed. Some of them circled back and followed the procession at a distance, ironically the same route as just days before this "Anointed One," as he was hailed, had been welcomed into the city with crowds, cheers and shouts of victory.

What went on inside the house of Annas and then afterwards in the High Priest's upper room, is well documented elsewhere but suffice it to say, it was a mock trial through and through, with false witnesses being brought forward with spurious lies, accusing the man of high treason, both against the Law of Moses and in contradiction of Caesar himself. By the third watch of the night, the bruised and bloodied country Preacher had all but been sentenced to death by the word of Caiaphas, who at one point ripped his tunic and exclaimed, "what more must we hear? From his own lips to our ears, he claims to be the Son of G-d! This is blasphemy!"

Now because it was not lawful by their own scriptures to put a man to death, they all arose together as the cock crowed a third time in the stillness of that morning hour and led him out to the Palace of the Governor of Judea, Pontius Pilatus.

# FRIDAY

The sun was just raising its head over the eastern horizon as the cacophony of collusion marched up the steps to the Portico of Pilate, demanding to be seen and heard, despite the early hour of the Shabbat Passover morning. It had not fully come yet, but it was the morning of, and in their minds, much needed to be done before sunset.

They would not enter the Governor's headquarters for fear of being defiled before eating the Passover feast so arousing Pilate was no easy task. However, they would not be denied.

"By the starry crown of Jupiter! These wretched people annoy me to no end!" Pilate shouted as he threw water on his face and gathered on a robe over his sleeping tunic.

"It is never-ending with them, first one problem then another, one uprising then another, one political... manipulation then another. Oh, to be in Rome again! Will they never give me rest?!"

Pilate's dresser servants did their best to appease him and hand him trinkets, jewelry, or an item of the breaking of fast, some cheese, a bit of pork, his laurel. He waved it all off in dramatic sweeping motions of his hands, and then on second thought, called back the servant with the embroidered wineskin and snapped his fingers repeatedly pointing to a goblet for a taste of uncut wine and honey to start the day.

Downing the wine in one swallow and immediately demanding another as he walked, he then finished it and threw the goblet against a corridor chair in a fit of minor, if not feigned outrage before two Royal Guards, who stepped into the tantrum and shadowed him on either side.

He paused before the double-doored entryway, breathed deep through his nostrils and blew out a thick exasperated breath out his mouth before giving a nod to the doorman to swing it open wide.

Without saying a word, Pilate surveyed the scene in front of him with an air of pompous bigotry and quickly deduced that this was simply a mob on a mission of death. He looked at the man bound by ropes standing in the middle, his robe already bloodied around his shoulders and sullied with dirt from more than one toss to the ground. Pilate lifted his chin to deliberately look down his broad nose upon the gathering, wrinkling his lips into a disgusted grin and saying, "what a fine collection of souls upon my portico this sunny Passover morning." He paused for effect.

"Now, what is the accusation you bring against this man you have before me?"

Caiaphas was the natural spokesman for the assembly, and he quickly answered him with a slight flippant bow.

"If this man were not doing evil among us we would not have delivered him over to you," he said. "He continually stirs up the entire city with his talk of kingship and forbids us even to pay tribute to Caesar."

Pilate raised his right eyebrow at this and indicated with a double beckoning of his fingers to his guards to bring the man into his headquarters.

"Send for Atticus," he said to one of the black-clad men, who whipped his fist to his armored chest and immediately left the premises.

Ω

Atticus was already up and awaiting news of the previous night's arrest. He was not expecting a Black Guard summons to Pilate's headquarters, however, and he wasted no time in responding.

In the time it took for Atticus and the guard to return to Pilate's house, the Governor had already questioned the Galilean carpenter and declared him innocent. He was back on the portico, this time with the bloodied Messiah man standing next to him and now facing his accusers.

Pilate saw Atticus approaching.

"I wash my hands of this affair," he said to the group of Jewish leaders as he doused his hands in a wash basin. "His blood be upon your heads."

Atticus stepped up the stairs and followed Pilate as he shook his hands of the water, grabbed a towel from his nearby servant and strode through the large pillared doors.

He stopped abruptly and turned to face Atticus.

"These people are insolent and dead set on crucifying this… this criminal… ha! I find no guilt in him. He may be a pretender, a false prophet perhaps, but he is no criminal."

"What happened my Lord?" Atticus asked.

"Oh, I had asked this Nazarene if he is indeed the King of the Jews… and he asked me a question! Me! He asked me whether I said that of my own accord. The nerve! He is a tricky one, that is for certain, my good Atticus." Pilate reached for another cup of cut wine and honey a servant held out to him, took a sip and continued.

"Am I Jew? I asked him that," he paused, laughing at his own brilliance. "He said that his kingdom is not from this world and when I prodded him saying, 'so you are a king then?' he said, it was for this reason he was born and for this purpose he has come into the world – to bear witness to truth."

The word "truth" hung in the air.

"Truth." Atticus said.

"That is exactly my thinking… I asked him, what is truth?

"And what did he say?"

Pilate took another sip of the watered-down wine and looked at it as if it did no good or was bitter.

"He said nothing. But I did not wait for an answer either. I went out and told the Jews that I found no guilt in him. That is when I remembered the custom of releasing a prisoner so I asked them if they wanted me to release their king to them."

"And?"

"NO! They did not want him released. They shouted that they have no king but Caesar! And they called for Barabbas! Barabbas! Crucify their Christ… can you believe that? That insurrectionist dog is the one they call for?! They call for his release? I don't understand them at all. But my word is my word."

One more sip. He put the silver goblet down on a ledge and shook his head to clear it of the matter.

"I ordered him flogged and my men took him away. I wash my hands of it. I do. The flogging should be enough."

Just then the Royal Guards returned with Yeshua through a side corridor, dragging him along. He had been beaten badly, barely conscious but still standing. Atticus grimaced. He had seen a lot of beaten men and blood did not disturb him. It was the backstory that he was still navigating in his own mind and why the need for such brutal treatment. They had thrown a purple robe on him and a crown of spiny branches from a Paliurus tree adorned his head. The green glossy leaves almost shone against the sweat and dark blood of this "King." The spikes were sharp as dagger points and had been driven into his flesh with a baton.

Pilate pointed to the portico and they half-dragged, half-carried him out to the crowd again, which had increased now to over a hundred. The eastern commander of 25 had moved his battalion between the mob and the stairs with full shields locked to prevent any approach up the portico.

"Behold the man!" Pilate cried out. When the chief priests and the officers saw him, they cried out, "Crucify him, crucify him!" and the rest of the crowd began to join in the chant.

Pilate shook his head again. He was confused and wanted nothing to do with this man. But he feared for his own position when the people called him no friend of Caesar's for not condemning the Nazarene to death. Bringing the accused back into his headquarters once more with Atticus following behind, he asked him where he was from, knowing of course that he was a Galilean. But the man just stood silent before Pilate.

So, Pilate raised his hand to his chin and asked, "how do you not speak to me? Do you not who I am? Who it is you are talking to? Do you not know I have authority to release you and to have you crucified?"

At that, Yeshua spoke. Through parched and stricken lips, the Nazarene said Pilate would have no authority over him at all, had it not been given to him from above.

Atticus was surprised, to say the least. Even in this state, the Preacher spoke with a grace and wisdom he had not heard before.

He had also learned that there had been a trial of sorts at Herod's that morning as well, and that Pilate and Herod had even mended their ways somewhat – an ongoing feud - in dealing with this supposed King. Apparently, Herod had found no guilt in him either.

Pilate paced, first four steps to the left then back again. "Scourge him," Pilate ordered his guards and they moved in obedience to their superior. The squad nearly lifted the prisoner and carried him out and down through the back stairs to the prison courtyard across the way.

To Atticus he said, "release the zealot. Give them what they want. The scourge will surely satisfy them."

Atticus tucked his right fist to his breastplate and departed the room through the same rear exit, down the stairs and across the straight road running north and south, where he ducked his head and entered the southern gate of the prison courtyard.

Ω

Today was Passover, so all three men were alert when the cell door opened, Jonas knowing the custom of release, Ethnan feeling ready as ever to change his situation, and Barabbas feeling nothing but hatred for the Romans and ready as ever to strike.

Barabbas strained against the lockdown of the leash and could feel the bolts loosening even further. Perhaps this was his heaven-sent opportunity, he thought. Perhaps soon the Phoenician would be dead, and he would be free.

However, it was not the Phoenician who entered. It was Atticus, dressed in full military garb, who stepped into the dampness of the cell, looking around with a sense of both disgust and perhaps even pity crossing his mind. He did not understand the feelings he was having these days and simply tried to bury them under duty. All this talk of the Messiah and love must be getting to him, he assumed.

"Barabbas" he said, commanding their attention. A Centurion rarely enters these doors.

Barabbas grunted as Jonas did his best to smile and cooperate, nodding in Barabbas' direction enthusiastically at the same time.

"For reasons I do not comprehend," said Atticus, "the gods have bestowed favor on you. You are being released now, out of the goodness of Governor Pontius Pilatus' heart. Hail Caesar."

"Well, hail Caesar indeed!" Barabbas shouted back with mock joy, as he stood upright. As he did so, the back slab of iron that held the chain to the wall broke loose and fell to the floor with the sound not unlike an anvil. Everyone in the cell just stood in silence looking down at it, including Atticus.

"We will need to get that fixed," said Atticus and pointed to the Phoenician to deal with it as he unlocked the leash around Barabbas' neck.

Barabbas rubbed his exposed skin at the release of the iron, and thought better of taking on a well-armed Centurion, especially since it appeared he was getting an armed escort out of this stinking jail!

As that thought dawned more fully on Barabbas, he growled to the Centurion, "what is all this about?"

"It is your Passover, Jew. It is the kindness of Pilatus to release you. You are free today."

"I am not arguing," he said with a grin. "See ya, boys!"

Jonas and Ethnan were standing in silence, even shock at the release of Barabbas. They said nothing.

The two men walked side by side, Centurion and murderer, unchained, and unbound, out through the corridors of the prison toward the sun-baked courtyard. Out toward freedom, thought Barabbas, smirking.

They came to an intersection of corridors, where the north and south met the east and west walkway. Approaching from the west was a small band of Royal Guards, and with them, the captive carpenter turned preacher being dragged along in the middle of the pack.

The two men stopped and let the procession go by.

Atticus looked at Yeshua and suddenly life slowed for him. He took in all the bruises, the blood, the brokenness. *This man had survived even the scourge,* he thought, and *that alone deserves respect*. It was not that common. The brutality of the Roman scourge, done that day at the hands of a Phoenician guard, could easily kill a man, and often did, ripping their skin from the bone and even exposing vital organs at times. They would tie the victim's hands to a ring taut above his head and pull him to his tip toes, stripping him of his clothes and then letting the barbarous scourge do its job. It didn't take long.

Barabbas also found he could not look away and stood there as the guards, six of them, held up and moved the Nazarene, step by step in the middle.

None of the guards noticed what happened next. Just as the group was passing, the Preacher-Teacher, Carpenter King, lifted his head and looked directly at Barabbas.

The intensity of his look could not be mistaken. Something was happening in it. Barabbas felt the Nazarene's eyes almost pierce his soul, for lack of a better word. And, he could not turn away even if he wanted to, but held his glance fast. And then the morbid parade rounded a corner and was gone into the darkness of the tunnel.

Barabbas and Atticus continued past the intersection and into the sunlight which caused them both to squint a little and shield their eyes. They continued side by side, across the scorched courtyard. Atticus unlocked the courtyard gate leading on to the street called Straight and said, "you are free today. Serve Rome."

Barabbas did not hesitate, gave a last look at Atticus and sprinted to the left, down the stone road.

Ω

Barabbas ran until he was out of breath. He had no coin nor purse to put it in, no sandals on his feet, only a ripped-up tunic that covered very little on the large man. He ducked into a doorway and caught his breath.

He could not believe his good fortune today. Set free! There is a G-d! he thought. He laughed out loud and looked up and down the street, which was jam-packed now of celebrants - Jews from afar and from within the city. He recalled days on the farm, celebrating Passover, in honor of when their Sovereign Yahweh had set the Israelite people free from the imprisonment of Pharaoh of Egypt. The thought crossed his mind -- the matchlessness of the moment –being set free on Passover just like his forefathers.

He had not known what his fate would have been had he attempted that escape or if he would have eventually starved in that hole. But, all in all, he was glad to be free. He looked again left and right, saw a distracted man trying to negotiate the purchase of two doves for a sacrifice, and moved in. The unsuspecting traveler would not know what hit him.

He stepped out and walked toward the stranger close enough to give him a good bump in the pressing crowd. The man excused himself with apology, only looking back briefly at Barabbas, before continuing his bargaining with the merchant.

Barabbas walked three more paces and smiled as he tossed the little coin bag six inches up and seized it out of the air again.

Things were in motion at the prison; something was happening. Ethnan and Jonas were backed into their corners in silence as Legionnaires came through the gates of the corridor, moving quickly and the Phoenician, back from his morning chore, opened the cell door.

"Up!" one soldier commanded and Jonas and Ethnan got up. They unlocked their chains and Jonas got out the word, "freedom?" before being slapped in the face by the soldier. It was obvious this was not the Passover custom.

The two were marched out and it soon became quite clear what was happening.

Jonas started screaming, "NO, NOOO!!" as he saw cross beams laid out on the street before him but the soldiers struck him and his cellmate into quick submission, ordering them both to pick up their cross and start walking.

A third man was already under the beam. Jonas did not recognize him. Ethnan cared less. All three were now in a parade of shame as the streets were lining up with people from all nations joining in a torrent of abuse hurled on the criminals.

Atticus pushed past the crowd and made his way back to Pilate's, taking the stairs in strides of two, before realizing that the Governor was watching from his balcony. He waved him in.

Upstairs, Atticus was shown into the living quarters and Pilate awaited him on the balcony overlooking the streets.

"It is happening, Atticus," he said. "I tried to let him go, had him beaten, had him scourged even ~ punished him to what I felt was sufficient ~ but no, it was not sufficient to them. I had him brought out to the Gabbatha (by this he meant the Stone Pavement) and they were calling for his crucifixion again. They called for his crucifixion! What could I do?"
Pilate was pacing like a tormented tiger in a cage. "I did not want a riot on my hands. Nor did I want Tiberius on my back. Therefore, I released him to their will. So, there it is," he added, pointing to the procession toward Golgotha, the place of the skull. "It is out of my hands now."

Atticus leaned out over the stretch of streets and could see the movement of bodies up the Via Doloroza, from which he had just made his escape.

"Listen to them, Atticus." Pilate stared out over the city. "Truly, it is as if they chose a revolution of hate, in preferring Barabbas... a revolution of hatred over a revolution of this man's message of peace and love..."

He thought about this for a moment before continuing. Now he was pensive, even, unusual for Pilate.

"You know my wife had a dream about him?"

"About the Jew?" Atticus asked.

"Yes, about this carpenter, teacher, whatever he is. She sent me a message during my talks with him that she had dreamt last night that I should have nothing to do with him, that I should not condemn him. She suffered much in the dream, it seemed."

"What do you make of it, sir?"

Pilate reflected on this question a moment, not looking at Atticus but still gazing out over the streets. He chose not to answer. Either he did not know, or he did know, but could not face it.

"I want you to oversee this crucifixion, Atticus. See to it. See that nothing else takes place today to upset the gods." And then he added, "...any more than has already taken place, that is."

Ω

Atticus knew what the streets would be like. The congestion would be worse than ever, now that a crucifixion march was happening. He knew the procession would be winding its way through the main streets to the Rock, the place of the skull, Golgotha. It was the way of it.

Mourners and rioters both, would be blocking almost every access, the rioters using every opportunity to create havoc, even the death of criminals, the mourners screaming out their opposition and desperation. Nothing and no one would stop the procession now; even Pilate was bound by his word.

It was near midday and the sun was high in the brilliant blue of the sky. Atticus would rather be somewhere else right now, but duty called. He chose to avoid the crowds altogether, by taking Tonitrua to Golgotha the longer way around, outside the city walls. He gathered what he needed, went to the stables, mounted and nudged his friend into action.

He marvelled at the training of this great horse and wondered who it was that spent so much time with him. Though a living being, the horse responded more like a machine, picking up every lean of Atticus' legs, whether to the right or to the left. It was almost as if Tonitrua could read Atticus' mind at times and responded accordingly up the steep hills.

Ω

Jonas was no longer in denial of his fate and his thoughts now were only for his family, his parents, his siblings. He scanned the crowd now and then looking for any familiar faces. There were none. Only anger and spitting hatred met his eyes, people lobbing vegetables and hurling curses upon him as he took up his cross. He was a dead man and he knew it. His mind screamed, "*why!*" but he knew why.

His life was racing before him now, past relationships, poor decisions, loves and losses. He fell under the weight of the crossbeam, got up quickly under the Roman whip. He felt pity for the man in front who had fallen twice already. It looked as if the one leading the procession had been severely flogged, likely the scourge, Jonas thought. He looked away, just trying to stay his mind on his own path in front of his feet. A woman came running out to give the man, her Leader, Messiah, King, a drink. He was a broken King now. King of fools, thought Jonas. A Legionnaire pushed her back. Jonas did not want to stumble again; he just wanted to get this miserable life of his over with. He even began to welcome death.

Behind him, Ethnan cursed back at the crowd when they threw insults in his direction. He walked slower than the others, due to his bad knee, but he did not care. The only thing that kept him moving forward was the leather strap of the Legionnaires, snapping against his back, his arms, and his legs.

Barabbas came out of a shop, wearing a newly purchased tunic and sandals, a leather vest and belt. He quickly took in what was happening, right in front of his eyes.

He watched in silence as the parade moved past him, realizing it was his own pathetic pair from the jailhouse, and the Nazarene Teacher.

He looked down at the street and a strange thought occurred to him.

*It should be me. This man is carrying the cross meant for me. It should be me in the middle of the street, being screamed at, carrying the means of my own execution, dying alone in so much humiliation.*

*He shook his head and closed his eyes, lifting his head back and opening his eyes to the blue sky above him. Why am I thinking in such ways, he asked himself. I am free. Free! Too bad for him. Too bad for that man.*

He looked back to the procession. What a way to die, he thought. *Give me a sword and I will fight to the death, or even kill myself before submitting to such humiliation. But this Teacher... he did not have a violent bone in his body and there he is, carrying my cross.*

Barabbas turned away and moved against the crowd, cutting into a back alley, north toward the highway. He needed to get out of this place and go back toward Magdala.

And then he saw her. He must be mistaken, he thought, but no, it was her. She was dishevelled; she was demoralized, but it was her. She was crying and pulling at her hair, but yes, it was her.

"Mariam!" he called out across the street. She could not hear him or did not want to.

"Mariam!" he pushed through the crowd easily to get to the other side. He paused just before reaching her, double checking his thoughts. Yes, it is her.

He grabbed her shoulder as she was looking away from him and breathed her name again.

"Mariam."

She turned in disbelief for that was all she could feel amidst her mourning, in the thick of her anguish. When she began to recognize him, his sheer size giving him away as the man from the Tavern a lifetime ago, she pulled back. She could not remember his name nor cared to. She turned back to the answer of her life, dying in the street.

"Mariam, it *is* you. What are you…" Barabbas was about to ask her the obvious but stopped. He drew closer to her but she paid no attention to him. Her eyes were on her Savior. Her heart was being wrenched out through her tears, as anger and angst, sorrow and bitterness all combined to produce unrestrained eruptions of emotion.

Barabbas had many thoughts running through his mind and stopped most of them from getting past his teeth. He decided to just move along with her and keep pace with the crowd, not looking at the criminals at all but keeping his eye on her. He stayed near. He would not lose her this time.

Ω

Tonitrua glistened with the salty sweat of the climb and almost seemed to gratefully nod at Atticus for the mat of fresh spring grass near the tether at the top.

Atticus scanned the hill called Golgotha, the appearance of it resembling a bony skeletal face. He looked skyward and appreciated the blue sky and hot sun on his brow.

Everything was ready. Pilate would be pleased. The stakes were in place, spikes and mallets at the ready. No ambushes in sight by insurrectionists. There would be no interference, no complications. All was ready. All he needed now were the ones to face their punishment.

The justice of Rome was quick and sure. No one escaped crucifixion, thought Atticus. No one survived. Criminals died by their own hand in one sense, the weight of their decisions and the weight of their body pulling down on the nails in such a way as to asphyxiate them. It was brutal, excruciating even, a word invented by historians to describe the act. No one could help them. They died alone.

Atticus did not like it, but he appreciated the thoroughness of crucifixion. If the convict did not suffocate quick enough, the soldiers simply broke their legs to prevent them from pushing up on the lower nail in the ankle and thereby gaining another breath. Once they could not push up, they would quickly lose the ability to breathe. They would die.

Only three today, he thought, but he had participated in hundreds of crucifixions, sometimes 20 or 30 in one day. Rome saw it as a deterrent to others when they lined the streets with the crucified, some at eye level, some lifted higher. Some were held by ropes; some were nailed with six-inch spikes through the wrists and feet; some received a combination of both rope and iron.

The vultures had begun to gather on the wall; Atticus looked at them with revulsion, not thinking so much about the winged creatures in the sky, though they were also circling overhead, familiar with crucifixions; no, he was eyeing the people, as sadistic early birds arrived. Atticus kept watch on them, with one eye on the Damascus Gate because he knew that it would not be long before the parade of souls would soon make their way through.

Still relatively early in the day, they came. The sound preceded them of course, clamouring and curses, dogs barking, the undistinguishable noise a crowd makes giving itself away as a mob. And then, the big gate swung open as his men led the way. Atticus wrinkled his nose up as he could almost taste the smell of death in the atmosphere. He noticed that some of the rabble had thinned now, gone on to other business of the day as Passover was dawning, but that the Pharisees were still there, some scribes, as well as the vultures as he called them, and then some mourners weeping for their Messiah, wracked in confusion and despair.

He moved into position at the top of the Rock where the re-usable holes had been dug for the large stakes to be dropped into. Even the dropping of the T-bar cross into the ground, added to the ripping pain of those being crucified.

The three were brought before him and dropped their heavy timber with a bouncing, echoing knock to the ground. All three also dropped to the ground themselves and instinctively tried to recover from their trek up the Doloroza. Atticus, though still fiercely loyal to Rome, found himself navigating thoughts of escape, retirement maybe, leave the military, go to Crete or Cyprus or even further, as far west as Spain. His mind was drifting, colourful sunsets, crystal water, sandy beaches... But he caught himself with wonderment, and pulled back into reality as the soldiers, some new recruits, were looking to him for instructions.

Atticus pointed to a broken, weeping Jonas and instructed his men to attach his wood to the stake on the left, a bit of a process of rope and iron, and the men moved on it quickly.

Again, Atticus nodded his instructions to do the same with the other two, and then things went fast. He dropped four spikes from his satchel on the ground in front of the men waiting with mallet in hand, and they went to work.

Jonas and Ethnan both reeled in their emptiness and yet strained and fought against the stronger soldiers in submitting to the cross. The Romans used a rope to pull Ethnan's right arm into spot as he was not giving in. They dislocated it in the process. No matter. He screamed out in new pain.

Atticus stepped back in disbelief when he watched Yeshua, unlike the other two, not resisting at all but crawling into position, slowly, painfully but willingly. It was almost like he was assisting the Romans in their cruelty. Atticus watched with furrowed brow.

Clouds began to gather in over Golgotha; hungry ravens were starting to gather nearby, squawking their approval.

Once the infantrymen finished their job of nailing the wrists and ankles into the wood, the crosses were raised via the ingenuity of a ropes-and-pulley system and dropped into the pre-made holes with a deafening trio of thuds.

And then it began. Then came the mocking, the jeering and outcry of hatred amidst ruined mourners, weeping at the foot of the Preacher, who was lifted up between the two thieves. Atticus heard Pharisees taunting him to save himself and prove he was Messiah. "Then we would believe you!" they shouted.

Atticus heard these things but was somewhere else, drifting far away to the west, to Spain. He was tired of this. Tired of bloodshed, tired of brutality, tired of Jerusalem. While he had participated in many crucifixions this was his first command over one, and it was taking its toll. He had to shake himself constantly to keep focused. Surveying the entire scene, listening to every word heaved upon the criminals, listening to their responses back, he was soaking it all in like one of the sponges laden with the sour wine they sometimes gave the victims.

When they would acquire their breath by standing up on the spike in their bloody feet, Ethnan and Jonas each screamed curses upon their executioners, as well as the crowd and their children's children for cutting his own life short. Ethnan would muster up all he had and hack spit toward the small gathering below him, and they made a game of it, dodging the spittle, laughing and bellowing, "missed! Try again!" He did not though, could not. He had dried up inside.

In the following hour, Jonas went silent, his mind swirled with the past, attempting to forget the present, and occasionally his thoughts would go to the future. What is next? So alone. No one here. No one at his bedside holding his hand as he expires in old age, no one able to wipe his brow or give him water. Utterly alone. That is part of the bane and shame of crucifixion, utter abandonment with absolutely no hope. He drifted away.


The morning waves of the Mediterranean lapped the shores of the beach where his father was preparing his boat for launch, moving and working as he talked to a 10-year-old Jonas.

"Abba, where do we go when we die?"

"Ha, son, that may be a question for the priest..." the weathered old man said, but as he looked at his boy, he thought better of delaying. His boy was a serious thinker.

"We Jews have One G-d as you know, Jonas; we follow Him. We trust Him. We trust Him to deliver us to paradise after we die, where life is far better than anything here."

Jonas pushed a hole in the sand with a stick, thinking life was good here, and why would one want to leave? "What is paradise?" he asked his papa.

Remembering the Hebrew scriptures instructing fathers to walk with their children and talk with their children about the God of their forefathers, he looked at his son with loving eyes and said, "son, paradise is... paradise is the presence of G-d."

The sound of the waves gave way to the sound of a Legionnaire yelling vulgarities. Jonas slowly opened his eyes and saw soldiers casting lots to the left of him, down below. One of them had just lost a seamless tunic that was once the Teacher's.

Atticus roamed through the crowd unhurriedly, trolling for any sound of trouble. There was none, other than the common abuse tossed upon those who were hung between heaven and earth. Each step Atticus took was deliberate and paced. He listened. He watched.

And He sighed deeply now and then.

He looked up quickly when the Hebrew Rabbi hanging there, lifted his voice, and roared, "Father! Forgive them! They know not what they do!"

A prayer of forgiveness was not unusual for dying men but praying for forgiveness for his abusers? This, Atticus had never heard before. He stared at the man as a soldier climbed a ladder and hung the inscription of his charge above him, nailing it in place with four hits of the mallet. The charge said, in Aramaic, Latin and Greek, "Yeshua of Nazareth, King of the Jews."

The Pharisees balked at this, saying it should read that he only *said* he was king of the Jews, but their words had no effect.

He stepped closer in, past a few of the followers. He listened to hear if this Messiah said anything else from his place above them all.

Atticus counted at least seven sayings the man uttered that day, including this prayer of forgiveness, strained through dried, parched lips. One was directed toward Jonas, who had called over to him, "Yeshua, remember me when you come into your kingdom!"

The Preacher turned and rested his cheek on his shoulder, causing little rivers of pain to shoot through his right arm. He winced, then looking him in the eyes, he said, "I say to you, truly, this day you will be with me in paradise."

Atticus watched as Jonas turned his head heavenward and even managed a smile, mouthing the word, "paradise" more than once. Relief. Peace. Atticus again marvelled at the power of this man's words.

Claps of thunder now rolled across the horizon as the sky darkened with speed - "the speed of a Roman warship" - Atticus would say in later days. The morning had gone quickly from a bright, sunny blue-sky day to storm clouds collecting in ominous purples, together over Golgotha at the sixth hour. He glanced toward his namesake of thunder - Tonitrua, stomping up and down, mostly toward three children who should have known better than to provoke the big horse. Atticus yelled at them, "Leave him!" They scattered.

Rain began, first in large droplets, then hard, pelting explosions of water, followed by full drenching, sideways rain. And the Preacher raised his voice again, lifting himself up on the spike despite the ripping agony and called out in a loud voice: "TETELESTAI!"

Atticus whispered the word out, "Finished." And then he watched as the once would-be King breathed deep again and exhaled, "Into Your hands, Father, I commit my spirit." He bowed his chin on his chest and breathed his last.

A huge crash of thunder punctuated his word and an earthquake began to roll over Golgotha as Yeshua expired. People screamed and ran for cover. Even the soldiers were taken off-guard and hung on to whatever they could, to steady themselves. Atticus did the same and grabbed hold of the foot of the cross below the dead man's feet until the rolling quake subsided.

He suddenly pulled away as he realized what he was holding onto.

The women wailed out a desperate cry heavenward and Atticus saw that Barabbas was one of the men standing near the mourners, doing his best to bring some sort of comfort to the women.

Standing at the foot of the cross, spear in hand, Atticus looked up at the Preacher and the words just tumbled out of his mouth in Latin and those closest heard it clearly, "Vere homo hic Filius Dei erat."

"Truly, this man was the Son of God."

Heaven began to empty itself of its storehouses and the rain poured down. Into the seventh hour of the day, it kept coming down. Atticus would learn afterward that the great curtain in the Jewish Temple, separating the people from the presence of God, had been ripped from top to bottom at the time of this sudden earthquake.

People took cover. No more crowd now, just the soldiers fulfilling their duty. Being the Jewish Day of Preparation for the Passover, rather than wait, Atticus gave the orders to break the legs and to get it done quickly. It was the lesser of two evils – letting them live longer and experience every painful moment of a slow death by suffocation, or snapping their legs so that suffocation comes swiftly. Atticus gave the order.

One or two hefty, rain-soaked blows with a mallet was all it took to each shin or kneecap, depending on who was given the task. For Jonas, it was the shins, and the agony overwhelmed him to the point of passing out from sheer pain. Death soon followed. Ethnan bellowed curses, as a young Legionnaire performed the horrid duty. He was dead before the soldier had moved the ladder down and made his way over to the final cross. The amount of stress on the man's heart and vital organs guaranteed a quick entry into the afterlife.

When they came to the Teacher, he seemed dead already to the soldiers' inspection – no signs of life. The Legionnaire looked at Atticus through the driving rain. Atticus tossed him his own spear and pointed to the torso of Yeshua. Obediently, the soldier drove the spearhead deep into the right side of the man's chest, and blood and water poured out.

Said Atticus: "He is dead."

# FRIDAY EVENING

Barabbas did his utmost to comfort Mariam of Magdala but his efforts were fruitless against the devastation of the death of her master. He tried his best but sensitivity and compassion did not come easy to him. They were not among his natural gifts.

She told him she needed to be alone and then went for a walk. Barabbas, meanwhile, was invited in to eat with her friends. Never one to turn down a meal, he simply went into the upstairs room. It was not a happy place. In fact, Barabbas did not need any sensitivity to pick up the shadowy feeling of death hanging over every person in every corner.

The people gathered there were sullen and only picked at the food. No one spoke except to comfort. Most just smiled a sympathetic smile at the other. There were two or three conversations that interested him, one about the fight in the Garden and how Shimon, the big fisherman, took a small sword to one of the Temple Guards. *Good for Shimon*, he thought, nodding his approval as he ate. These men, though, including Shimon, were full of fear and despair. All their hopes and dreams of the last three years of walking with their Messiah – whom they thought was the Messiah – had now come crashing down today with his death.

A man named Bartholomew spoke up, "but did not he talk about this – that he would suffer at the hands of the Pharisees and even die, and then rise again?"

Barabbas lifted his head from his plate to hear any response on this. Rise from the dead?

"He said it," Bartholomew said again, but no one was engaging. He returned to silence.

Another speaker was a man Barabbas recognized as being a known tax collector, or who once was a tax collector - *now a travelling preacher man, I guess*, Barabbas reckoned.

Matthew was pushing his hands through his hair. "Yes. He said it. He said it in many ways, that he would die, be murdered. We thought it was some sort of parable or something – not that it would really happen. Now he is gone."

That hung in the air as Barabbas took another piece of chicken, and then some bread which he dipped into olive oil before taking a bite.

"Tell me more about this leader," he said, wanting the conversation to stay as far away from himself as possible. But it did not work.

"Barabbas, was it not you they cried out to release, instead of Yeshua? Yes, yes, you were let loose this morning, were you not?" asked Bartholomew.

Barabbas stood up from the table immediately, anticipating a fight and took a defensive position. "I never asked for that! I never asked for any of this! I did not know what was happening! What of it? What do you want from me?" he asked, clenching his fists.

"Easy, big fella," said Bartholomew, "I just wondered if you realized that he took your place."

"I did... I do," Barabbas said and sat back down. "What can I say? What can I do about it? Nothing."

"Have you given any thought to the fact that Yeshua became like you... so that you might become like him?"

Bartholomew's question caught Barabbas by surprise. He did not know how to respond.

Ω

Pontius Pilate had just seated himself down peacefully at his dinner table when the delegation was shown in. It was nearing sundown and Pilate was finally putting the day behind him. But others were not. Now, Pilate breathed deeply and prepared himself for whatever was coming next.

His name was Joseph. He slowly walked into the room. He was a man of good standing from Arimathea. Pilate knew of him, and that he even had sway with the Sanhedrin, the assembly of 71 throughout every city in Israel, or Palestinia as the Romans knew it. He was known as a disciple of

Yeshua the Messiah, the one who had just been crucified.

"Yes?" Pilate did not look up from his dinner.

"With gratefulness," Joseph humbly requested the body of his dead leader and to have it straightaway, before the sun set, knowing the Passover Shabbat was about to begin. He desired to give him a decent, righteous burial. Joseph was a wealthy man with a large garden that had a new tomb cut out of a rock in the middle of it. It was to be his own tomb, but he now wanted to use it for the Nazarene as a gift.

"Atticus." Pilate waited for his Centurion to step to attention. "You oversaw the crucifixion. There are times when these criminals will last for days on the tree. What say you? Was the man dead or was he still fighting for his life when you left the hill?"

With a slight bow of his head, Atticus addressed his Governor with the greatest respect, saying, "Yes sir, we ensured all those crucified today had indeed died of their wounds. I assure you fully, my lord, that it was my own spear that was thrust into his heart."

"Very well, upon your word." Looking at the man from Arimathea, he took a sip of wine, smacked his lips and said, "You may have your body. Now let me eat my supper in peace, please!" And he waved Joseph away, who left quickly and joined a friend, one Nicodemus, in taking down the body and preparing it for burial with a 75-pound mixture of spices, myrrh and aloes. They bound the body in a linen cloth, as is the custom of the Jews, set him in the tomb, and rolled a great set stone against the entrance. Mariam Magdalena and another Mariam were also there at the tomb, watching all this.

Later that evening, Nicodemus was walking from the garden tomb, making his way past the Temple, when a thought struck him and nearly took his breath away.

It was an old Messianic scripture from the prophet Ysha'yah, which when translated, read, *"And they made his grave with the wicked and with a rich man in his death, although he had done no violence, and there was no deceit in his mouth."*

Nicodemus stopped walking and caught himself, put his left hand out to lean against the outer wall of a courtyard, his right hand over his mouth. He looked up at the full moon occupying the night sky as the Pesach, the Jewish Passover began. He whispered, "The Lamb of G-d that takes away the sin of the world..."

It was in the fourth watch of the night that Atticus awoke. It had been a fitful sleep at best and now he was sitting on the edge of his bed.
He could not escape the previous day's crucifixion. The words the Nazarene called out – "Forgive them," "It is Finished," then simply dying when he

wanted to, committing his spirit to his Father - all these things kept coming back to him.

Atticus decided then and there to resolve his troubled mind once and for all. He would search out Nicodemus again in the morning and speak with him once more about this Messiah. *But wait, how could a dead Messiah mean anything at all? He is dead! Does it – his life, his message -- not all collapse, now that he is dead?* He groaned as he lay back down on his bed and reflected on these thoughts and more. He prayed to Mars to give him rest; none came.

And he needed to talk with Pilate.


Barabbas could not sleep either. He was staying with the men of Yeshua, stretched out on a mat on the floor, as were the lot of them. Some of them stirred now and then but his eyes would not even close, despite his efforts to sleep.

His mind went back over the last days – his time in the cell, seeing Mariam, watching the crucifixions up close, seeing Jonas and Ethnan get their just rewards and realizing that he also should be the one up there. Bartholomew's comments… the thoughts just kept swirling around in his mind persistently.

He had never heard the Nazarene speak. Not once. He had never seen him heal anybody, yet somehow he was being drawn to him through his followers.

He kept thinking, *"my cross," "my death," "my penalty."* But those thoughts led him nowhere as there was no resolve to be found. It only left him with emptiness because one question that could not be answered still lingered: what was he supposed to do about it now?

He got up and quietly lifted the latch of the door. He needed fresh air, to walk, and maybe, if possible, to open a conversation with G-d that was long overdue. He had not spoken with G-d for years, and G-d had not spoken with him. There was much to discuss.

# SATURDAY

Shabbat.

Atticus could not find Pilate.

He searched for him at the Governor's Headquarters, at the stables, the baths, even in the prison, though he knew he would not be in there. None of the servants knew where he was, nor did any of the Royal Guard whom Atticus queried.

He was about to leave the headquarters and head up to the Cardo market when the laurel-wreathed man came parading up the street with an entourage of black-clad warriors. He was dressed in his royal red and white, looking quite pompous, even for him, thought Atticus, who wondered what his liege was up to, since it was the Jewish Shabbat and the streets were all but empty this morning.

"Felt the need to be among the people," said Pilate. "The city is pleasant and calm. Well done yesterday, Atticus. All seems well."

Atticus bowed as Pilate passed him up the portico stairs, knowing the calm was due only to the Shabbat.

"If I may have a moment of your time, sir," Atticus followed Pilate up the steps.

Pilate stopped at the top and adjusted his red cape. "What is it?"

"Sir, I would like to request a leave. I would like to take ship to Spain and plan for… for my retirement from the military."

Pilate wrinkled his long nose up at the request. "Very bold of you, Atticus. Were you not promoted to Centurion only days ago?! Yes, I believe I am correct!" he said quite arrogantly. "Now you are talking of retirement?"

Atticus bounced back quickly, apologetically. "Oh, not retirement for many years sir, no, just some time away… for planning. Securing some land perhaps."

"Hmm. My answer is no, Atticus. That will be all." And then he added, "I will give it more thought tomorrow, perhaps."

Atticus bowed again, raised his right fist toward his heart but Pilate had already turned away and went through the doors. Atticus did not finish the salute.

Ω

Barabbas was treasuring the brilliance of the morning rays of the sun, sitting at a little table halfway out into the Cardo. Shops were not open. He had been giving much thought to his plans now that he was truly a free man. He still harboured ill will against Rome, no question, but wondered at the futility of insurrection. The might of Rome was indeed daunting. And… and, he was free! No longer a price on his head. He thought of Mariam, of course, and wondered where she would be today, whether she would be leaving for Magdala soon. Perhaps he would join her, if she would have him. He decided to return to the upper room where his newly acquired friends, the followers were hiding, knowing that she would be sure to return there today at some point to continue their mourning together.

He rose.

Ω

M ariam wept.

Her soul was filled with sorrow at the loss of the Master. How could this have happened? All the plans and hope for the future, the building of his kingdom… everything she was believing for was gone.

Her tears kept coming. She wrapped herself in mourning black and sat on a three-legged stool at the Jerusalem home of her dear friend Ioanna the wife of Chuza, an important court official for Herod Antipas. Ioanna was employed as a steward of the house of the Tetrarch in the Galilee as he was known, and had met Yeshua early on in his ministry. Antipas gained notoriety when he put to death the prophet Yochanan, also called the Immerser, by the sword.

The meaning of her own name, however, is "Yahweh has been gracious" and according to her, He certainly had! She had been set free from her many infirmities when she met the Teacher on the shores of Capernaum and was a strong supporter and follower ever since. As the wife of one of Herod's most important court officials, she had the means to travel with and to contribute to the ministry of Yeshua for the last three years.

"Mariam…" Ioanna spoke her name through her own tears. "Oh, he loved you so."

"He loved all people."

"Yes, but he held a special place in his heart for you. What are we going to do now, Mariam? I mean besides returning to our former life without him…"

"I cannot go back to my former life," said Mariam. "I can never go back to Magdala; it is too painful, too many bad memories." She wiped her eyes, to no avail. "I know he would not want us to be crying so much. Did you hear him on the road, on the Doloroza? He said to us, 'daughters of Jerusalem, weep not for me."

"How can he be… just gone?" asked Ioanna. "It does not seem real. Not even a week ago, people were shouting his name in the streets and calling for him to save them!"

Mariam got up and walked to a nearby window, looked out over the southern slopes of the city, the terraced gardens, the houses on the hills. Her eyes brushed over Gethsemane, the garden where he would go to pray, where he was betrayed, where he was arrested and taken captive, and brought to his death.

"I need to go to the tomb," she said. "I want to take some myrrh… and aloes… anoint his body."

"I will go with you," Ioanna answered with a leap in her voice. "I have much myrrh in my storehouse."

"We will go in the morning." Mariam spoke with authority. "It is more than a Shabbat's walk for us today, but we can prepare today to go tomorrow. No one will see us in our preparations," she added, knowing that the Pharisees do not view lightly those who break Shabbat.

# SUNDAY MORNING

The legal record will say that Atticus' men had fallen asleep on the job in the middle of the night, and that the followers of Yeshua had come, removed the large stone that blocked the grotto in the rock, and silently stole the body, leaving behind the burial cloths and the napkin which had lain on the face of their Master, neatly folded at the head of the stone slab.

By mid-morning there was no small commotion among them all -- the Temple Guards, the Royal Guards, the Pharisees, the Sadducees, the Scribes, Rulers and any other city official one could think of.

Yeshua of Nazareth was missing.

For the Sanhedrin, 'the thing they feared the most had come upon them' as the historical wisdom book, Job, records. Much to the consternation of his enemies, it appeared that word that was spreading quickly that Yeshua may have indeed risen from the dead – pure rubbish in their minds -- but something that needed to be quashed as soon as possible.

Unofficially, Atticus questioned his men thoroughly of course, and was absolutely satisfied that they were lying through their teeth. No Roman infantryman would ever be caught dead sleeping on the job. In fact, they would be dead if they were caught in such a manner! And it would not be a quick death, either, thought Atticus – he had seen more than one soldier die by fire, and that fire was lit with the flame of his own clothes in a pile at his feet as he stood naked, tied to a stake. It was most degrading for a Roman citizen. It was severe, almost as bad as crucifixion but Romans were not allowed to be crucified.

"They must have been paid a substantial sum of silver," Atticus mused to himself, because they were staying with the story. He was not going to push it even though the men seemed... frightened in some way, he thought. Pilate seemed unwilling to pursue it so the whole matter was dropped rather quickly. Atticus was more interested in personally investigating this so-called resurrection, or to find the body and prove it wrong.

From what he understood so far, the Teacher had appeared to some women that morning – and "why would his followers make that up?" he wondered, standing on his beloved terrace overlooking the city. He was alone and looked around to see if anyone was taking note of him talking to himself. He liked to work things out in his mind this way.

"If his followers were lying, if they had truly stolen the body and were now falsifying information to fabricate a fable of their teacher rising from the dead, why would they use women as their first witnesses? Women are not worth listening to in trial; they are not believed at the best of times; they are not even educated. Why not say that it was one of their leaders that saw him? One of the fishermen maybe? Or the tax collector. That would be more believable."

"Unless, of course… no," he turned his gaze to the Mount of Olives. "Unless of course, it is actually true. But it cannot be so. No one lives after crucifixion. No one. It is impossible."

The streets were beginning to awaken; the sound of sheep, the smell of the animals, dogs, people, the din of it all rose to Atticus' veranda. He leaned over to see two men running. He recognized them as two of the followers. It looked like a race, one in front of the other, dodging in and out of people and carts, sheep and goats, running hard.

"I wonder where they are off to…" Atticus watched until they were out of sight, trying to piece it together, when the women came around the corner. He steadied his birds' eye view as they also ran by his dwelling, going in the same direction as the men.

"Interesting. Time to go."

Just then a hammer-like pounding confronted his door. He turned quickly, picked up his dagger and moved to the entryway.

Ω

Big fishermen generally do not run, and that was Shimon's excuse for losing the footrace to the garden tomb that day. Yochanan, who would later write a detailed account of that morning (as history is often written by the victors, they say), was first at the sepulchre.

Shimon, also known as Cephas, would eventually laugh off the contest but he was not laughing at the moment. Confusion, fear and shame were the ruling triad in his mind as he pulled up at the open tomb, his lungs about to burst out of his chest. The great stone that had enclosed the cave was now a good deal away from the resting track it had lain in. It stood some two Roman paces away, still on its end but up against an olive tree. How it got there, no one knew; even three strong men could not have rolled it that far.

Yochanan was slowly standing up from walking out of the cave hewn into the rock when Shimon arrived.

"It is a miracle," he said trying to gather his thoughts, as Shimon approached and bumped him aside, entering the tomb himself. What he saw there was very little. The reason they were even there was because Mariam had come in exasperated that morning and told them she had seen the Lord. Shimon stood up inside the cave, adjusting his eyes. The grave shroud lay on the stone bed as if it had just been rolled off by a waking son on a chilly morn; the napkin that covered the face was folded up at one end, where the head would have been. Shimon stared into the candle-lit darkness, running through several scenarios in his mind.

The most obvious was that someone took his body, grave robbers perhaps, but that did not make sense; there was nothing in here to take. But then who? The Jews? (By this he meant the Council of the Sanhedrin). But they feared him, so why would they take his body and give credence to his teachings? The Romans? Again, why? Grave robbers… his mind went to them again. Why would they take the time to fold the face cloth? Why would they not have taken the burial shroud, at least that would have brought a good coin? The candle light flickered as others were arriving and moving the air as they entered the small enclosure. He turned and made his way out, while those entering asked him, "where is he? Where is he, Shimon?"

"I do not know," he said, and grunted acknowledgements to others but inside, his mind was still racing. Yochanan believed the Master had risen.

"What do you make of it?" he asked Yochanan looking intently in his friend's eyes for truth.

"He spoke of it… often," said Yochanan. "He said he would suffer, and die and rise again, but we did not know what he meant. Did not believe him. I do not know, Shimon, but if this truly has happened, this will change everything. Some things are starting to make sense now. We must go and tell the others."

Shimon followed in step but spoke nothing. He was still thinking of the night of the betrayal – of Judas' kiss in the garden, but more of his own betrayal in denying that he even knew Yeshua when questioned by a little girl.

He was still reeling from the shame of that moment, and of how he had told Yeshua that not only would he never deny him, but that he would even go to death for him that very day! Such failure, he thought. Such failure! How could I deny even knowing him?

The scene rushed back at him; they had gone to the Garden because the Master wanted to pray, and that was his favorite place of prayer. He recalled being so tired that night, falling asleep several times before the sound of soldiers' feet and the light of the torches roused him fully awake. In the chaos of those moments and in the dancing light of the torches, he found himself reacting like the old Shimon, drawing his scaling knife and slicing an ear from a man's head. Yeshua had simply picked it up and put it back on!

Then his night had turned into a nightmare as the Teacher was dragged away. Shimon had followed at a distance and watched as his Master was beaten before him and pulled into the house of Annas. He went to a nearby courtyard, and was warming himself by a fire when a servant girl recognized him as one of the disciples. The first denial came quickly, out of his mouth before he had time to even think. It was an act of fear, of self-protection in saying, "no I never knew him."

But the second and third denial, he could not deny were thought out! They were calculated, the third coming with a curse even. Oh, how he hated himself now! What a wretched man I am! He beat himself inside his head, loathing his own thinking as he brought back that dreadful night. And then the horrible rooster crowed and he remembered the words of the Master, "by the time the cock crows you will have denied me thrice."

"Never… I said - never!" Shimon shook his head and spoke it out in disbelief now. Yochanan only looked at him, patted him on the shoulder and said, "let us run, brother."

He broke off at a quick pace, and Shimon, looked up, breathed deeply and put himself to the pace. "I hate running!" he shouted after Yochanan.

Ω

Mariam looked him in the eyes and tried to explain.

"I am already taken. I have given my entire life over to Yeshua. I thought he was dead. Now I know he is alive. I will serve him with an undivided heart all of my days."

Barabbas tried to comprehend her words. The Messiah is now alive? This was difficult to believe. All that the disciples had told him about Yeshua's teaching, his message of love, had made no change in him at all, because... well look where it had gotten him - the man was now dead! But, now... Mariam's words brought new thoughts, new hope to him – if he was risen like she said - then what Bartholomew had told him takes on new meaning as well.

If Yeshua had died in his place on that cross, taking the punishment that was meant for him, and dying in his stead – and if he really rose again... why, that would mean his debt is more than paid in full on earth. It would mean paid in full before G-d! He would in truth be a free man. He could not be tried again for crimes already served here and the same would be applied eternally. And if Yeshua rose from the dead, does that not prove that everything he said was therefore true? If, if, if! Did he? Did he rise? If only he could see this risen Messiah, he too like Mariam would serve him with his whole life, what a revolution that would be... he pondered the thought.
"I am trying to understand," he told her. "Saddened that you would choose another man over me... but

if that is the way of it, I am glad that it would be him over any other."

Ω

Atticus did not sheath his dagger before opening the door but quickly did so when he saw that it was a member of the Royal Guard. He swung the door open.

"A message from Pilatus sir," the guard dipped his chin in respect to Atticus and held out his right hand.

In his hand, a rolled note. Atticus took it, nodded thanks and said that he would respond. The guard left him to the note as Atticus closed the door.

He walked back toward the terrace, unravelling the scroll as he stepped out into the sunlight.

*Atticus Cornelius Julianus*
*I have reviewed your request for absentia in Spain and have decided to keep to my pronouncement of refusal. However, I have graciously decided to redeploy you to the shores of the Great Sea in the development of the port city, Caesarea. You will remain under my command and I have allotted you 100 men of the Italian Cohort. Report at*

*once to Caesarea. I will see you next when I am back at my home there in a fortnight.*
*For the Glory of Rome*
*Pontius Pilatus*

Atticus sat down on a bench and considered this news. His life had dramatically changed in just one week, from a Commander of 50, to Centurion of the Third in Jerusalem, to Centurion of the Italian Cohort at Caesarea. He looked at the note in his hand, rolled it up and whispered, "hail Caesar…"

# Epilogue

When we last left Barabbas, he was navigating the waters between doubt and belief, questioning whether the Messiah had really risen from the grave or not. If he had, he would serve him, if not, he would continue to be a plague to the Romans and the Roman Empire.

It would be a revolution for him one way or the other, one of violence or one of love.

Though it is not recorded in the books of history, the following is one account passed down through the generations.

Barabbas met the risen Savior. He was in a crowd of some 500 people who saw him on a hillside of the Kinneret, almost a month after the crucifixion and various appearances. He was on the hill, a natural amphitheatre, teaching the people just like He always did. Following the sermon that morning, Barabbas knelt on the grassy slope and committed his life to following the Master, renouncing the sword and the evils of this world and to forever follow the Christ. Mariam was there. But she was not part of his decision that day, except to join in the call to be about advancing His rule and reign throughout the entire earth.

Barabbas returned to his father's house while he was in the Galilee, seeking reunion and restoration.

Every step of the way, he would rehearse in his mind what he would say.

"Father, I have sinned against heaven and against you. I am not worthy to be called your son. Treat me like a servant. I will serve you all the days of my life as a hired hand."

But while still afar off, his father saw him coming. He could not believe his eyes; he ran around in a small circle as he thought about what to do! Then he did what no respectable Jewish man his age would do. He hiked up his robes and ran out to meet his boy, embracing him with a multitude of kisses on his face and neck.
His son, who was dead, was now alive again.

He worked on the estate for the next ten years, until his father went the way of his ancestors. He too, had become a devout follower of Yeshua. Barabbas and his older brother even hosted a gathering in their home every week in honour of the Messiah.

By all accounts, Barabbas would become a respected man and a confident preacher of the good news of a risen Savior. He carried a life-message of how one man's cross became Another's, and how the death of the One had brought him life to the full.

Ω

Atticus spent the next decade at Caesarea Maritima, a calming presence in a bustling and rapidly growing city dedicated to its namesake, Caesar Augustus. Herod the Great had built the city in honor of the Caesar and it was very much a Roman city, complete with hippodrome, public baths, amphitheatre and even a grand temple to the gods. Many Centurions retired to Caesarea for its beautiful beaches and opulent lifestyle.

Atticus, known then, by his second name, Cornelius Julianus of Caesarea, was much loved by the people of the city, both Roman and Jew, Scythians, Cretans and Greek. His experience with the crucifixion of the Christ had changed him that third day of April, 33 A.D. He felt if Yeshua was indeed the Son of God, he would be wise to seek out more of this Yahweh, which he did. He feared the Jewish Deity, prayed to Him daily, and tried to live the best he could, in honor of Him. His former god, Mars was simply gone from his mind.

One day in 43 A.D. he had a vision as is recorded elsewhere:

"At Caesarea, there was a man named Cornelius, a centurion of what was known as the Italian Cohort, a devout man who feared God with all his household, gave alms generously to the people, and prayed continually to God. About the ninth hour of the day he saw clearly in a vision an angel of God come in and say to him, "Cornelius." And he stared at him in terror and said, "What is it, Lord?" And he said to him, "Your prayers and your alms have ascended as a memorial before God." (Acts 10:1-5 ESV)

He was instructed by the "man in shining clothing," as he called him, to send for a fisherman named Shimon, who was staying at the house of a tanner in Joppa, and to request that he come to his house and tell him all that the Lord would command him.

So, Atticus – Cornelius – did as he was instructed and sent a devoted soldier and two servants down to Joppa to fetch this man, Shimon, whom he had never met personally.

Shimon came to the house of Cornelius and beginning with the baptism that Yochanan had proclaimed in the desert, he told of all the happenings in Judea and Jerusalem right up until the crucifixion and resurrection.

Atticus lowered his head when Shimon said, "They put him to death on the tree… as was ordained by G-d the Father – who then raised him up again, and we are all witnesses of this and testify to the saving power of Yeshua and that He is the one who will judge the living and the dead."

While he was still speaking, this G-d of the Hebrews sent a mighty rushing wind into and through Cornelius' house and what was known as the Holy Spirit fell upon them all, filling them with such a presence and confirming to them all that Shimon was indeed telling them the truth. It marked the first time that the news of Yeshua had crossed over from the Jews to all the other nations – known as the Gentiles.

Atticus became a devout follower of Yeshua all the days of his life, including on all his travels east and south into Africa.

He never did make it to Spain. But that is another story.

Ω

*The End*

~

Made in the USA
Columbia, SC
08 July 2017